C#

PROGRAMMING

C# Programming

C#

PROGRAMMING

A Step-by-Step Guide for Absolute Beginners

BRIAN JENKINS

C# Programming

Bestselling Book in Python programming from the same author

C# Programming

Edited and Published by

ATS Coding Academy and Amazon Kindle Publishing

© Copyright 2019 by Brian Jenkins.

All rights reserved.

C# Programming

By reading this document, the reader agrees that under no circumstances is the author responsible for any losses, direct or indirect, which are incurred as a result of the use of information contained within this document, including, but not limited to, errors, omissions, or inaccuracies.

Thank you!

Thank you for buying this book! It is intended to help you to start coding with the powerful C# language.

C# Programming

C# Programming

Book Objectives

The following are the objectives of this book:

- To help you understand the origin of C#.

- To help you know how to get started with C# programming by setting up the coding environment on various operating systems.

- To help you understand the syntax and constructs that make up the C# programming language.

- To help you transition from a C# Beginner to a Professional.

- To help you learn how to develop a complete and functional computer application with C# on your own.

Who this Book is for?

The author targets the following groups of people:

- Anybody who is a complete beginner to C# programming or computer programming in general.

- Anybody in need of advancing their C# programming skills.

- Professors, lecturers or tutors who are looking to find better ways to explain C# to their students in the simplest and easiest way.

- Students and academicians, especially those focusing on computer programming and development of Softwards.

What do you need for this Book?

For Windows users, install the following:

- Microsoft .Net Framework.

- Microsoft Visual Studio.

For Linux and Mac OS users, install the Mono framework.

What is inside the book?

The content of this book is all about C# programming. It has been grouped into chapters, with each chapter exploring a different feature of the C# programming language. The author has provided C# codes, each code performing a different task. Corresponding explanations have also been provided alongside each piece of code to help the reader understand the meaning of the various lines of the code. In addition to this, screenshots showing the output that each code should return have been given. The author has used a simple language to make it easy even for beginners to understand.

About the Author

Dr. Brian Jenkins has a Ph.D. in computer science. He conducted coding research for magnetic recording systems and long-haul fiber optic communication systems. With two decades experience teaching programming to newcomers, and one of the most talented IT specialists of his generation, Dr. Brian works as a Research Software Specialist and occasional as a bioinformatician. Brian has been in the software field for over 20 years and explored implementations of the Prolog language, and over his career has worked as a professional software developer on compilers, programming tools, scripting systems, and assorted client/server and business applications.

In addition, Brian worked as a research and teaching assistant at the Chair of Information and Coding Theory (ICT) towards his Ph.D. degree at the Faculty of Engineering.

Since 2015 Brian resides in Geneva, in Switzerland with his wife, and daughter. He is working on series of books in programming and data science.

C# Programming

"Good programmers use their brains, but good guidelines save us having to think out every case."

Francis Glassborow

C# Programming

C# Programming

Introduction

C# is one of the many object-oriented programming languages that we have. The language is multi-purpose; hence we can use it to develop various types of applications. C# is popular for its syntax which is easy for one to grasp. This has made it one of the best coding languages for absolute beginners to computer programming.

C# was developed by Microsoft. This might make you think you can only code in C# on the Windows operating system. This is partially true as C# requires the .Net framework which can only run on the Windows operating system. However, there are alternatives to the .Net framework which you can use to write and run C# programs on other operating systems like Linux and Mac OS. This book helps you understand everything about C# including its origin, setting up the environment and writing and executing your C# programs. Enjoy reading!

C# Programming

To my wife Chelsea and my daughter Britany

You are the happiness of my days, and you are my truest love!

C# Programming

C# Programming

Table of Contents

C# Programming

Chapter 1- Getting Started with C#

A brief Overview of C#

C# is a powerful object-oriented programming language that was developed by Microsoft. We can use C# to develop various types of applications including windows, web, console and other types of applications using Microsoft Visual Studio. C# was developed during the development of .Net framework by Anders Hejlsberg together with his team.

The Environment

A number of tools are required for C# programming. Note that C# is part of the .Net framework and it is used for development of .Net applications. It is good for us to explore the relationship between C# and .Net framework.

The .Net Framework

The .Net framework is a platform for software development developed by Microsoft. The framework was created for development of applications that can run on the Windows platform. Its first version was released in 2002 and given the name .Net framework 1.0. Since then, a lot of updates have been made on the framework up-to-date.

C# Programming

We can use the .Net Framework for creation of both web-based and form-based applications. We can also use it to develop web services. Other than C#, the .Net framework also supports the visual basic programming language. This means that the programmer has the option of choosing the language in which to develop their application in.

IDE (Integrated Development Environment)

An IDE is a program that allows you to write your program. Most .Net developers prefer using Visual Studio Community as the IDE. It allows you to create, debug and run your applications. This IDE can be used for development of both web-based and form-based applications. To use this IDE, you must download and install it on your computer. You can find it in the URL given below:

https://www.visualstudio.com/downloads/

You are allowed to choose between the Visual Studio Community Forum, which is free, and Visual Studio Professional Edition, which comes with a 30 day trial period, and after the expiry of that period, you must pay for it.

C# Programming

Once the download is complete, double click the setup file to begin the installation of visual studio. Follow the on-screen instructions until the installation of visual studio is complete.

After that, you will be ready to start creating your own C# applications.

C# on Linux and Mac OS

The .Net framework only runs on Windows. However, there are alternatives that can run other operating systems like Linux and Mac OS. A good example of this is Mono, which is an open source edition of .Net framework capable of running on various operating systems including the many Linux distributions and Mac OS.

Hello World

Let bus create the "Hello World" example in C# to demonstrate how C# works:

Begin by creating the workspace. To do this, follow these steps:

- Launch Visual Studio.

- On the menu bar, select File -> New -> Project.

- Select Visual C# from templates, and then select Windows.

C# Programming

- Select Console Application.

- Type a name for the project then click OK button.

- This will create a new project in the Solution Explorer.

- Write your code in Code Editor.

Add the following code to the code editor:

```
using System;
namespace HelloWorld {
   class Hello {
      static void Main(string[] args) {
/* Our first C# program */
         Console.WriteLine("Hello World!");
         Console.ReadKey();
      }
   }
}
```

To run the code, just click the Run button or press the F5 key and the project will be executed. The code should return:

```
Hello World!
```

The code begins with the *using* statement. What this statement does is that it adds the *System* namespace into the program. C# programs normally have multiple *using* statements.

In the next line, we have a *namespace* declaration. A namespace is simply a collection of many classes. Above, we have the *HelloWorld* namespace in which we have the *Hello* class.

In the next line, we have the class declaration. The *Hello* class has method and data definitions that the program will be using. A class normally has numerous methods. The purpose of a method is to state the behavior of a class. However, our *Hello* class above only has one method, the *Main* method.

In the next line of code, we have the definition of the *Main* method, which marks the entry point for all for C# programs. It is the Main method that states what happens after execution of a class.

Next, we have the */* ... */* line. This is a comment, and the C# compiler will ignore the line. The line is only meant to increase the readability of the code by human readers.

Next, we have the *Console.WriteLine(...)* line. WriteLine is a method of the Console class that is defined in the System namespace. This line will print the *Hello World!* message on the screen.

Lastly, we have the *Console.ReadKey();* statement. This line is for *VS.NET* users. The line will make the program to wait for a key press and prevent the screen from running then closing quickly once the program has been launched from the Visual Studio .NET.

Other than running the program from the Visual Studio, it is possible for you to run a C# program from the command prompt of the operating system. To do this, follow these sequences of steps:

- Open your text editor then add the code given above to it. An example of a text editor is Notepad.

- Save the file with the name *helloworld.cs*

- Launch the command prompt of the operating system then navigate to the directory you have saved the file.

- Type the command *csc helloworld.cs* on the prompt then press the enter key to compile the code.

- If the code has no errors, the command prompt will take you to next line then generates the file *helloworld.exe*. This file has executable code.

- Type *helloworld* on the prompt to execute the program.

- The output *Hello World!* Will be printed on the screen.

Chapter 2- Data Types

C# is a strongly typed language; hence it expects you to state the data type any time you are declaring a variable. Let us explore some of the common data types and how they work:

1. bool- this is a simple data type. It takes 2 values only, True or False. It is highly applicable when using logical operators like *if* statement.

2. int- this stands for *integer*. It is a data type for storing numbers with no decimal values. It marks the most popular data type for numbers. Integers also have several data types within C#, based on the size of the number that is to be stored.

3. string- this is used for storage of text, which is a sequence of characters. C# strings are immutable, meaning that you cannot change a string once it has been created. If you use a method that changes a string, the string will not be changed but instead, a new string will be returned.

4. char- this is used for storage of a single character.

5. float- this is a data type used for storage of numbers that have decimal values in them.

The *sizeof()* method allows us to know the size of a variable or data type. The size is returned in the form of bytes. Consider the following example:

```
using System;
namespace TypeApp {
    class IntType {
        static void Main(string[] args) {
            Console.WriteLine("Size of int: {0}",
sizeof(int));
            Console.ReadLine();
        }
    }
}
```

The code should return:

```
Size of int: 4
```

Which means that an integer takes a storage size of 4 bytes?

Chapter 3- Variables

A variable is simply a name that is assigned to a storage area. Our programs are capable of manipulating such a storage area. Each C# variable is associated with a type which determines the amount of space allocated to that variable in the memory. This also determines the kind of operations that can be applied on the variable. For example, you cannot multiply string variables.

In C#, the following syntax should be used in variable declaration:

```
<data_type> <variable_list>;
```

The *data_type* in the above syntax must be a valid data type in C# like an int, String, float etc. The *variable_list* can be many variable names separated using commas. Below are examples of valid variable declarations:

```
int a, b, c;
char c, d;
float x, salary;
double y;
```

A variable can be initialized during its declaration. For example:

```
int x = 40;
```

C# Programming

Variable Initialization

Variable initialization refers to the process of assigning a value to a variable. In C#, this is done using an equal sign then followed by constant expression. Here is the general syntax for initialization:

```
variable_name = value;
```

As we had stated earlier, variables can be initialized during their declaration. Here are more examples:

```
int x = 1, y = 6;      /* initializing x and y. */
byte f = 22;           /* initializes f. */
double pi = 3.14159;   /* declaring an
approximation of pi. */
char a = 'a';          /* the variable a has a
value of 'a'. */
```

Variable initialization should be done correctly; otherwise, the program may give unexpected results. For example:

```
using System;
namespace VariableDeclaration {
   class MyProgram {
      static void Main(string[] args) {
         short x;
         int y ;
         double z;
         /* actual initialization of variables */
```

C# Programming

```
        x = 5;
        y = 10;
        z = x + y;
        Console.WriteLine("x = {0}, y = {1}, z
= {2}", x, y, z);
        Console.ReadLine();
    }
  }
}
```

The code returns the following:

```
x = 5, y = 10, z = 15
```

Getting User Input

The Console class of the System namespace has a method named *ReadLine()* that allows us to get input from the user. The user's input is read and stored in a variable. The following example demonstrates how to use this method:

```
using System;

namespace UserInputApp
{
    class MyProgram
    {
        static void Main(string[] args)
```

```
    {
            string firstName = "Nicholas";
            string lastName = "Samuel";


            Console.WriteLine("Your name is: " +
firstName + " " + lastName);


            Console.WriteLine("Please enter a
different first name:");
            firstName = Console.ReadLine();


            Console.WriteLine("Your new name is:
" + firstName + " " + lastName);
            Console.ReadLine();
    }
    }
}
```

When prompted to enter a new value for first name, do so and hit the enter key. You will realize that your name has changed.

C# Programming

Chapter 4- Type Conversion

Type conversion refers to the process of converting a value from one data type to another data type. It is also referred to as Type Casting. In C#, this takes two forms:

- Implicit type conversion- such conversions are done by C# in a type-safe way. A good example is a conversion from a smaller to a larger integral type or a conversion from a derived class to a base class.

- Explicit type conversion- such conversions are done by the users explicitly using some pre-defined functions. A cast operator is required for the explicit type conversions.

Here is an example of performing an explicit type conversion:

```
using System;
namespace ExplicitTypeConversionApp {
  class ExplicitTypeConversion {
    static void Main(string[] args) {
      double x = 2356.62;
      int y;

      // cast double to int.
      y = (int)x;
      Console.WriteLine(y);
```

```
        Console.ReadKey();
    }
  }
}
```

The code returns the following result:

```
2356
```

First, we had a double data type. However, we have converted it into an integer in the following line:

```
y = (int)x;
```

That is why the result is an integer.

There are various type conversion methods provided by C#. They include the following:

- ToBoolean- converts the type to Boolean if possible.

- ToByte- converts a type to byte.

- ToChar- converts to single UNICODE character if possible.

- ToDateTime- converts a type (string or integer type) to date time structures.

- ToDecimal- this method converts an integer or floating point value to a decimal type.

C# Programming

- ToDouble- the method converts the specified type to a double.

- ToInt16- this will convert a type to 16-bit integer.

- ToInt32- the type will be converted to a 32-bit integer.

- ToSbyte- this method will convert a type to a signed byte type.

- ToSingle- the methods converts a type into a small floating point number.

- ToString- this method converts a type into a string.

- ToType- this method converts a type into a specified type.

- ToInt64- the type will be converted to a 64-bit integer.

Consider the example given below in which the various types are converted into strings:

```
using System;
namespace TypeConversionApp {
   class ConversionToString {
      static void Main(string[] args) {
         int x = 53;
         float y = 41.007f;
         double z = 1645.4651;
```

```
        bool b = false;
        Console.WriteLine(x.ToString());
        Console.WriteLine(y.ToString());
        Console.WriteLine(z.ToString());
        Console.WriteLine(b.ToString());
        Console.ReadKey();
    }
  }
}
```

The code returns the output given below:

```
53
41.007
1645.4651
False
```

C# Programming

Chapter 5- Operators

Operators are symbols that instruct the compiler to perform a certain logical or mathematical manipulation. C# has a wide variety of operators. Let us discuss them.

Arithmetic Operators

These are used for performing various mathematical operations. They can be used as shown in the following example:

```
using System;
namespace AithmeticOperatorsApp {
    class MyProgram {
        static void Main(string[] args) {
            int x = 31;
            int y = 10;
            int z;
            z = x + y;
            Console.WriteLine("1: - z equals to
{0}", z);
            z = x - y;
            Console.WriteLine("2: - z equals to
{0}", z);

            z = x * y;
```

C# Programming

```csharp
        Console.WriteLine("3: - z equals to
{0}", z);

        z = x / y;

        Console.WriteLine("4: - z equals to
{0}", z);

        z = x % y;

        Console.WriteLine("5: - z equals to
{0}", z);

        z = x++;

        Console.WriteLine("6: - z equals to
{0}", z);

        z = x--;

        Console.WriteLine("7: - z equals to
{0}", z);

        Console.ReadLine();

    }

  }

}
```

Most of the above operators are well known except for a few of them. The ++ is the increment operator and it increases the value of the variable by 1 for each iteration. The – is the increments operator and it decrements the value of the variable by 1 after each iteration. The % is known as the modulus operator and it returns the remainder after division. The code returns the output shown below:

```
1: - z equals to 41
2: - z equals to 21
3: - z equals to 310
4: - z equals to 3
5: - z equals to 1
6: - z equals to 31
7: - z equals to 32
```

Relational Operators

C# supports a number of relational operators. The purpose of these operators is to compare values. This way, you can check the relationship between any two values during programming. The following code demonstrates how to use the various relational operators:

```csharp
using System;
class MyProgram {
    static void Main(string[] args) {
        int x = 31;
        int y = 10;
        if (x == y) {
            Console.WriteLine("1: x is equal to y");
        } else {
            Console.WriteLine("1: x is not equal to y");
        }
        if (x < y) {
```

```csharp
        Console.WriteLine("2: x is less than
y");
      } else {
        Console.WriteLine("2: x is not less
than y");
      }
      if (x > y) {
         Console.WriteLine("3: x is greater
than y");
      } else {
        Console.WriteLine("3: x is not greater
than y");
      }
      /* Let us change the values of x and y */
      x = 10;
      y = 30;

      if (x <= y) {
        Console.WriteLine("4: x is either less
than or equal to y");
      }
      if (y >= x) {
        Console.WriteLine("5: y is either
greater than or equal to x");
      }
   }
}
```

C# Programming

The code returns the following when executed:

```
1: x is not equal to y
2: x is not less than y
3: x is greater than y
4: x is either less than or equal to y
5: y is either greater than or equal to x
```

The == is the equal to operator, and it checks whether the values are equal top each other or not. The < is the less than operator, > the greater than operator. The <= is the less than or equal to operator while >= is the greater than or equal to operator.

Logical Operators

C# also has number logical operators. Let us discuss them briefly:

1. Logical AND (&&)- the condition is true if both operands are nonzero.

2. Logical OR (||)- the condition is true if any of the operands is nonzero.

3. Logical NOT (!)- the operator reverses the logical state of an operand. If the condition is true, this operator will make it false.

The following example demonstrates how to use the above operators:

```
using System;
namespace LogicalOperatorsApp {
    class MyProgram {
        static void Main(string[] args) {
            bool x = true;
            bool y = true;
            if (x && y) {
                Console.WriteLine("1: The condition
is True");
            }
            if (x || y) {
                Console.WriteLine("2; Thecondition
is True");
            }
            /* let us change the values of  x and y
*/
            x = false;
            y = true;
            if (x && y) {
                Console.WriteLine("3: The condition
is True");
            } else {
                Console.WriteLine("3: The condition
is not True");
            }
            if (!(x && y)) {
                Console.WriteLine("4: The condition
is True");
```

C# Programming

```
        }
        Console.ReadLine();
    }
  }
}
```

The code returns the following output:

```
1: The condition is True
2; Thecondition is True
3: The condition is not True
4: The condition is True
```

Assignment Operators

C# assignment operators can be used as demonstrated in the following example:

```
using System;
namespace AssignmentOperatorsApp {
    class MyProgram {
        static void Main(string[] args) {
            int x = 31;
            int z;
            z = x;
            Console.WriteLine("1: =  The value of z
is = {0}", z);

            z += x;
```

```csharp
        Console.WriteLine("2: += The value of z
is = {0}", z);


        z -= x;
        Console.WriteLine("3: -= The value of z
is = {0}", z);
        z *= x;
        Console.WriteLine("4: *= The value of z
is = {0}", z);


        z /= x;
        Console.WriteLine("5: /= The value of z
is = {0}", z);
        z = 100;
        z %= x;
        Console.WriteLine("6: %=  The value of
z is = {0}", z);
        z <<= 2;
        Console.WriteLine("7: <<=  The value of
z is = {0}", z);
        z >>= 2;
        Console.WriteLine("8: >>=  The value of
z is = {0}", z);
        z &= 2;
        Console.WriteLine("9: &=  The value of
z is = {0}", z);
        z ^= 2;
```

```
        Console.WriteLine("10: ^= The value of
z is = {0}", z);

            z |= 2;

        Console.WriteLine("11: |= The value of
z is = {0}", z);

        Console.ReadLine();

    }

  }

}
```

The code returns the following result:

```
1:  =  The value of z is = 31
2:  += The value of z is = 62
3:  -= The value of z is = 31
4:  *= The value of z is = 961
5:  /= The value of z is = 31
6:  %=  The value of z is = 7
7:  <<=  The value of z is = 28
8:  >>=  The value of z is = 7
9:  &=  The value of z is = 2
10: ^= The value of z is = 0
11: |=  The value of z is = 2
```

C# Programming

Chapter 6- Conditional Statements

C# has conditional statements, mostly used for con trolling the flow of execution. The conditional statements expects the programmer to specify a condition or a set of conditions and the corresponding set of statements to be executed if a condition is found to be true. The programmer can also specify the set of statements that are to be executed if the condition is not true.

Let us discuss the various conditional statements supported in C#.

if Statement

This statement is used to evaluate a Boolean expression before a set of statements can be executed. If the condition is true, then one set of statements will be executed, otherwise, another set of statements will be executed. Here is the syntax for this statement:

```
if(boolean_expression) {
    /* statement(s) to execute if above boolean
expression is true */
}
Here is an example:
using System;
namespace DecisionMaking {
    class IfStatement {
```

```
        static void Main(string[] args) {
            /* defining a local variable */
            int x = 5;
            /* check a boolean condition via if
statement */
            if (x < 10) {
                /* to be printed of the condition is
true */
                Console.WriteLine("x is less than
10");
            }
            Console.WriteLine("The value of x is :
{0}", x);
            Console.ReadLine();
        }
    }
}
```

The code returns the following output:

```
x is less than 10
The value of x is : 5
```

The condition was found to be true, that is, the value of variable x is less than 10, hence, and the statement just below the condition was executed. What if the condition was false?

```
using System;
namespace DecisionMaking {
```

```
class IfStatement {
    static void Main(string[] args) {
        /* defining a local variable */
        int x = 15;
        /* check a boolean condition via if
statement */
        if (x < 10) {
            /* to be printed of the condition is
true */
            Console.WriteLine("x is less than
10");
        }
        Console.WriteLine("The value of x is :
{0}", x);
        Console.ReadLine();
    }
}
```

The code returns the following:

```
The value of x is : 15
```

The condition was found to be false, hence the statement outside its

block was executed.

if-else Statement

This is simply a combination of an *if* statement with an *else* part. The *if* part is executed if the condition is true, while the *else* part is executed when the condition is false. The two parts cannot all be executed at once. Here is the syntax for the statement:

```
if(boolean_expression)
{
// code to be executed if condition is true.
}
else
{
// code to be executed if condition is false
}
```

Consider the example given below:

```
using System;

namespace DecisionMaking {
    class IfElseStatement {
        static void Main(string[] args) {
            /* defining a local variable */
            int x = 5;

            /* a check of the boolean condition */
            if (x < 10) {
```

```
        /* if the condition is true, the
following will be printed */
        Console.WriteLine("x is less than
10");
    } else {
        /* if the condition is false, the
following will be printed */
        Console.WriteLine("x greater than
10");
    }
        Console.WriteLine("The value of x is :
{0}", x);
        Console.ReadLine();
    }
  }
}
```

The code returns the following:

```
x is less than 10
The value of x is : 5
```

The *if* condition evaluated to a true, hence the statement within its block has been executed. What if the condition was false?

```
using System;
namespace DecisionMaking {
    class IfElseStatement {
        static void Main(string[] args) {
            /* defining a local variable */
```

```
        int x = 15;
        /* a check of the boolean condition */
        if (x < 10) {
            /* if the condition is true, the
following will be printed */
            Console.WriteLine("x is less than
10");
        } else {
            /* if the condition is false, the
following will be printed */
            Console.WriteLine("x greater than
10");
        }
        Console.WriteLine("The value of x is :
{0}", x);
        Console.ReadLine();
    }
}
}
```

The code gives the following output:

```
x greater than 10
The value of x is : 15
```

The *if* condition evaluated to a false, hence the statement within the *else* block has been executed. You must have noticed that part outside the two blocks has been executed in both cases. That is what happens.

else…if Statement

In some cases, we may be in need of checking a multiple number of conditions. In such a case, we can use the *else if* statement. It takes the syntax given below:

```
if(boolean_expression a) {
    /* Runs if the boolean expression a is true */
}
else if( boolean_expression b) {
    /* Runs if the boolean expression b is true */
}
else if( boolean_expression c) {
    /* Runs if the boolean expression c is true */
} else {
    /* to run if none of above conditions is true */
}
```

Here is an example:

```
using System;

namespace DecisionMaking {
    class ElseIfStatement {
        static void Main(string[] args) {
```

```csharp
        /* defining a local variable */
        int x = 5;


        /* checking the boolean condition */
        if (x == 1) {
            /* print this statement if the
condition is true */
            Console.WriteLine("Value of x is
1");
        }
        else if (x == 2) {
            /* print this statement if the if
else if condition is true*/
            Console.WriteLine("Value of x is
2");
        }
        else if (x == 3) {
            /* print this statement if the if
else if condition is true */
            Console.WriteLine("Value of x is
3");
        } else {
            /* print this statement if none of
the above conditions is true */
            Console.WriteLine("All conditions
are false");
        }
```

```
        Console.WriteLine("Exact value of x is:
{0}", x);
        Console.ReadLine();
    }
  }
}
```

The code prints the following result:

```
All conditions are false
Exact value of x is: 5
```

All the conditions were found to be false; hence the block of code outside the conditions has been executed. Let us set the value of variable x to 2 and see what happens with the code:

```
using System;
namespace DecisionMaking {
    class ElseIfStatement {
        static void Main(string[] args) {
            /* defining a local variable */
            int x = 2;
            /* checking the boolean condition */
            if (x == 1) {
                /* print this statement if the
condition is true */
                Console.WriteLine("Value of x is
1");
            }
```

```
        else if (x == 2) {
            /* print this statement if the if
else if condition is true*/
            Console.WriteLine("Value of x is
2");
        }
        else if (x == 3) {
            /* print this statement if the if
else if condition is true */
            Console.WriteLine("Value of x is
3");
        } else {
            /* print this statement if none of
the above conditions is true */
            Console.WriteLine("All conditions
are false");
        }
        Console.WriteLine("Exact value of x is:
{0}", x);
        Console.ReadLine();
    }
  }
}
```

The output is shown below:

```
Value of x is 2
Exact value of x is: 2
```

C# Programming

An *else if* condition evaluated to a true hence the statement within its block was executed. The block of code outside all the conditions was also executed. You can play around with the code by modifying the value of x to various values and see what will happen.

Nested if Statements

C# allows us to nest conditional statements. We can nest both the *if* and the *else if* statements, which means that we use them inside another *if* or *else if* statement. The following syntax demonstrates how we nest the *if* statement in C#:

```
if ( boolean_expression a) {
    /* to execute if the boolean expression a is
true */
    if (boolean_expression b) {
    /* to execute if the boolean expression b is
true */
    }
}
```

The *else if* statement can be nested using the syntax given above.

Consider the example given below:

```
using System;
namespace DecisionMaking {
    class NestedIf {
        static void Main(string[] args) {
```

C# Programming

```
        //* defining local variables */
        int x = 1;
        int y = 2;


        /* checking the boolean condition */
        if (x == 1) {
            /* if the condition is true, check
the if condition below */
            if (y == 2) {
            /* if the condition is true,
print the following */
                Console.WriteLine("Value of x is
1 and b is 2");
            }
        }
        Console.WriteLine("Exact value of x is
: {0}", x);
        Console.WriteLine("Exact value of y is
: {0}", y);
        Console.ReadLine();
    }
  }
}
```

The code returns:

```
Value of x is 1 and b is 2
Exact value of x is : 1
Exact value of y is : 2
```

Both *if* conditions evaluated to a true, hence the statement within the nested *if* were executed. If either or both conditions evaluated to a false, then this statement could not have been executed. Here is an example:

```csharp
using System;
namespace DecisionMaking {
   class NestedIf {
      static void Main(string[] args) {
         //* defining local variables */
         int x = 1;
         int y = 2;
         /* checking the boolean condition */
         if (x == 1) {
            /* if the condition is true, check
the if condition below */
            if (y == 3) {
               /* if the condition is true,
print the following */
               Console.WriteLine("Value of x is
1 and b is 2");
            }
         }
         Console.WriteLine("Exact value of x is
: {0}", x);
         Console.WriteLine("Exact value of y is
: {0}", y);
```

```
        Console.ReadLine();
    }
  }
}
```

In the above code, the nested *if* condition checks whether the value of variable y is 3, which is false. The statement within this block will not be executed. The C# compiler will skip this section and proceed to execute the code outside the conditions. It returns the following:

```
Exact value of x is : 1
Exact value of y is : 2
```

switch Statement

This statement is the same as using multiple *if* statements. It is created with a list of possibilities, an action for every possibility and a default section to be execution in case any of the options doesn't evaluate to a true. Here is syntax for this statement:

```
switch(expression)
{
    case <value_1>
        // code
        break;
    case <value_2>
        // code
```

```
        break;
    case <value_N>
        // code
        break;
    default
        // code
        break;
}
```

Here is an example:

```
using System;
public class SwitchStatement
{
        public static void Main()
        {
int a = 3;
switch (a)
{
    case 1:
        Console.WriteLine("The value of x is
1");
        break;
    case 2:
        Console.WriteLine("The value of x is
2");
        break;
    case 3:
```

```
        Console.WriteLine("The value of x is
3");
        break;
    default:
        Console.WriteLine("Unknown value of x");
        break;
    }
  }
}
```

The code returns the following:

```
The value of x is 3
```

The value of variable was initialized to 3. After executing the code, the *case* code for 3 will be matched, hence the statement within its block will be executed. If none of the *case* conditions is true, then the *default* section will be executed. This is demonstrated below:

```
using System;

public class SwitchStatement
{
        public static void Main()
        {
int a = 5;
```

C# Programming

```
switch (a)
{
    case 1:
        Console.WriteLine("The value of x is
1");
        break;
    case 2:
        Console.WriteLine("The value of x is
2");
        break;
    case 3:
        Console.WriteLine("The value of x is
3");
        break;
    default:
        Console.WriteLine("Unknown value of x");
        break;
    }
  }
}
```

The code returns the output given below:

```
Unknown value of x
```

The case label within the switch statement has to be unique. The switch statement is usable with expressions of any type including strings, integers, bool, char, enum rtc. Here is how to use it with a string:

```csharp
using System;
public class SwitchStatement
{
        public static void Main()
        {
string firstName = "Nicholas";
switch (firstName)
{
    case "Samuel":
        Console.WriteLine("Your first name is Samuel");
        break;
    case "Nicholas":
        Console.WriteLine("Your first name is Nicholas");
        break;
    case "Bismack":
        Console.WriteLine("Your first name is Bismack");
        break;
}
    }
}
```

The code returns the following output:

```
Your first name is Nicholas
```

Goto in switch

In some cases when using the *switch* statement, we may need to skip to a certain case. This can be done using either a *jump* or *goto* statement. Consider the example given below:

```csharp
using System;
public class SwitchStatement
{
      public static void Main()
      {
string firstName = "Nicholas";
switch (firstName)
{
    case "text":
        Console.WriteLine("is your first name");
        break;
    case "Samuel":
        Console.WriteLine("Samuel");
        break;
    case "Nicholas":
        Console.WriteLine("Nicholas");
        goto case "text";
        break;
```

```
    case "Bismack":
        Console.WriteLine("Bismack");
        break;
}
    }
}
```

The code returns the following output:

```
Nicholas
is your first name
```

Nested Switch

A switch statement can be created within another switch statement. This gives us a nested switch. Here is an example:

```
using System;
public class NestedSwitch
{
        public static void Main()
        {
                int x = 10;
                switch (x)
                {
                        case 10:
                                Console.WriteLine(10);
                                switch (x - 1)
```

```
            {
                    case 9:

        Console.WriteLine(9);
                        switch (x
- 2)
                {
                                case
8:

        Console.WriteLine(8);

        break;
                            }
                        break;
                }
                break;
            case 20:
                Console.WriteLine(20);
                break;
            case 125:
                Console.WriteLine(25);
                break;
            default:
                Console.WriteLine(30);
                break;
        }
```

```
        }
}
```

The output is as follows:

```
10
9
8
```

Chapter 7- Loops

Looping is the ability to repeat the execution of a block of code for a number of times. This is a popular technique in programming. Generally, statements are executed in a sequential manner. There are various types of loop supported in C# that allow us to control the execution paths. Let us discuss these:

while Loop

This is the simplest loop in C#. It works by executing a block of code provided the provided condition is true. It takes the following syntax:

```
while(condition) {
    code block;
}
```

The code block in the above case can have a single or multiple statements. The loop will iterate through the code block provided the condition is true. Here is an example:

```
using System;
namespace LoopsApp
{
    class WhileLoop
    {
```

```
        static void Main(string[] args)
    {
        int x = 0;
        while(x < 5)
        {
            Console.WriteLine(x);
            x = x + 1;
        }
        Console.ReadLine();
    }
}
```

The code prints the following results:

```
0
1
2
3
4
```

The value of variable x was first initialized to a 0. The while condition checks whether the value of this variable is less than 5, meaning that the 5 itself is not included. In the statement $x = x + 1$, we want the counter to increase the value of x by 1 after every iteration. After the 4th iteration, the program finds itself violating the *while* condition (x should be less than 5), hence it halts execution.

C# Programming

A *break* statement can be used inside a *while* loop. For example:

```csharp
using System;
public class WhileLoop
{
        public static void Main()
        {
                int x = 0;
                while (true)
                {
                        Console.WriteLine("x is: {0}", x);

                        x++;

                        if (x > 5)
                                break;
                }
        }
}
```

The break commands the compiler to stop execution when it realizes that the value of x is greater than 5. The code returns the following:

```
x is: 0
x is: 1
x is: 2
x is: 3
x is: 4
x is: 5
```

We can also nest a while loop, whereby we create a while loop inside another while loop. For example:

```csharp
using System;
public class WhileLoop
{
    public static void Main()
    {
        int x = 0;
        while (x < 2)
        {
            Console.WriteLine("x is: {0}", x);
            int y = 1;

            x++;
            while (y < 2)
            {
                Console.WriteLine("y is: {0}", y);
                y++;
            }
        }
    }
}
```

C# Programming

The while loop for the y variable is nested inside the while loop for variable x. The code prints the following:

```
x is: 0
y is: 1
x is: 1
y is: 1
```

for Loop

This loop is applied when the programmer knows the exact number of times for which they need to execute a block of code. The loop has the following syntax:

```
for (initialization; condition; increment)
{
    //code block
}
```

The code block will be executed until when the condition evaluates to a false. The *initialization* allows us to initialize the loop variables. These loop variables are updated by the increment.

For example:

```
using System;
namespace LoopsApp
{
```

```
class ForLoop
{
    static void Main(string[] args)
    {
        int a = 5;
        for(int x = 0; x < a; x++)
            Console.WriteLine(x);
        Console.ReadLine();
    }
}
}
```

The code returns the following:

```
0
1
2
3
4
```

The value of variable "a" was initialized to 5. In the *for* loop, we have used the condition that the value of x is less than the value of "a". This means that the loop will execute from the initial value of x at 0 to 4, and then it halts execution. The reason is because for $x=5$, it will be violating the loop condition that $x<a$.

We can create an infinite *for* loop, which means that the loop will run forever. This occurs when we don't specify the initialization, the

C# Programming

condition or the increment part. Top avoid this, always that the condition part of the loop returns a false at some time, after which the execution of the loop will halt. Here is an example of an infinite *for* loop:

```
for ( ; ; )
{
    Console.Write(0);
}
```

The code will print 0 forever.

We can use a *break* statement to exit from a *for* loop. For example:

```
using System;

public class ForLoop
{
    public static void Main()
    {
        for (int x = 0; x < 10; x++)
        {
            if( x == 5 )
                break;

            Console.WriteLine("x is: {0}", x);
```

```
                }
            }
}
```

Here is the output from the code:

```
x is: 0
x is: 1
x is: 2
x is: 3
x is: 4
```

We have used a *break* statement to stop execution of the loop when the value of x is 5.

We can also nest a *for* loop, in which we will create a *for* loop inside another *for* loop. For example:

```
using System;
public class NestedForLoop
{
        public static void Main()
        {
                for (int x = 0; x < 5; x++)
                {
                        for(int y =x; y< 4; y++)

        Console.WriteLine("Value of x: {0}, Y: {1}
", x,y);
                }
```

C# Programming

```
        }
}
```

Here is the output from the code:

```
Value of x: 0, Y: 0
Value of x: 0, Y: 1
Value of x: 0, Y: 2
Value of x: 0, Y: 3
Value of x: 1, Y: 1
Value of x: 1, Y: 2
Value of x: 1, Y: 3
Value of x: 2, Y: 2
Value of x: 2, Y: 3
Value of x: 3, Y: 3
```

The *for* loop for the variable "y" has been nested inside the *for* loop for variable "x".

do…while Loop

This loop is closely related to the *while* loop, with the main difference being that the evaluation of the condition is done after the loop has been executed. This means that there is a guarantee that the code block has been executed for at least once.

The loop takes the following syntax:

```
do
{
        // code block
```

```
} while (boolean_expression);
```

Here is an example:

```
using System;
public class DoWhileLoop
{
        public static void Main()
        {
                int x = 0;

                do
                {
                        Console.WriteLine("x is: {0}", x);
                        x++;
                } while (x < -1);
        }
}
```

In the above case, the value of x has been initialized to 0. However, this violates the *while* condition, which states that the value of x should be below -1. However, this condition will be evaluated after the code block has been executed; hence the execution will run for only once before halting. The code returns the following:

```
x is: 0
```

To make the loop execute for a number of times, we can modify the code to the following:

```csharp
using System;
public class DoWhileLoop
{
        public static void Main()
        {
                int x = 0;
                do
                {
                        Console.WriteLine("x is: {0}", x);
                        x++;
                } while (x < 5);
        }
}
```

The loop will execute from the value of x at 0 to 4 to return the following result:

```
x is: 0
x is: 1
x is: 2
x is: 3
x is: 4
```

A break can also be added inside a *do...while* loop as follows:

C# Programming

```csharp
using System;
public class DoWhileLoop
{
        public static void Main()
        {
                int x = 0;

                do
                {
                        Console.WriteLine("x is: {0}", x);
                        x++;
                        if (x > 4)
                                break;
                } while (x<10);
        }
}
```

The *break* statement helps us break from executing the loop when the value of x is greater than 4. This means that the code block will be executed from the value of x equals 0 to 4. Here is the output from the code:

```
x is: 0
x is: 1
x is: 2
x is: 3
x is: 4
```

C# Programming

Also, a *do...while* loop can be nested inside another *do...while* loop. The following example demonstrates this:

```csharp
using System;
public class NestedDoWhile
{
        public static void Main()
        {
                int x = 0;

                do
                {
                        Console.WriteLine("x is: {0}", x);
                        int y = x;

                        x++;

                        do
                        {
                                Console.WriteLine("y is: {0}", y);
                                y++;

                        } while (y < 2);
```

```
        } while (x < 2);
    }
}
```

The code returns the following:

```
x is: 0
y is: 0
y is: 1
x is: 1
y is: 1
```

foreach Loop

This type of loop is used for iterating through a collection of items such as arrays and other built-in list types. Let us use an ArrayList, which is a simple list, to demonstrate this:

```
using System.Collections;
using System;
namespace LoopsApp
{
    public class ForEachLoop
    {
        public static void Main()
        {
            ArrayList ls = new ArrayList();
            ls.Add("Nicholas Samuel");
            ls.Add("Michelle Nic");
```

C# Programming

```
        ls.Add("Jane Boss");
        foreach(string name in ls)
            Console.WriteLine(name);

        Console.ReadLine();
        }
    }
}
```

The code returns the following result:

```
Nicholas Samuel
Michelle Nic
Jane Boss
```

C# Programming

Chapter 8- Methods

A method is simply a group of statements that have been put together to perform a common task. Every C# class has at least one method, which is the Main method. For you to be able to use a method, you must define it, and then call it to perform the action it was intended to perform.

Method Definition

A method definition is simply a declaration of the elements that form the structure of the method. Here is the syntax for method definition in C#:

```
<Access_Specifier> <Return_Type>
<Method_Name>(Parameter_List) {
    Method Body
}
```

Let us define all the meaning of the above elements:

- Access Specifier- this will determine how visible a method is from other classes.

- Return type- it is possible for a method to return a value. The return type is simply the data type of the return value from the method. If the method is not expected to return any value, it should be declared as void.

- Method name- this is a unique identifier for the method, and it is case sensitive. The method name should not be the same as any other identifier that has been defined in the class.

- Parameter list- the purpose of parameters is to send and receive data from a method and they are enclosed within parenthesis. The parameter list denotes the type, the order and the number of parameters of the method. Note that the parameters are optional, meaning that a method may be created with no parameters.

- Method Body- this is a set of instructions that are required to complete a required activity.

Consider the following example:

```
using System;
using System.IO;
class NumberChecker {

    public int CompareValues(int x, int y) {
        /* Declaring a local variable */
        int answer;

        if (x > y)
            answer = x;
        else
            answer = y;
```

```
      return answer;
   }


}
```

We have just defined a function that checks named *CompareValues* that takes in two integer values then it compares them to return the larger of the two. The access specifier has been set to *public*, meaning that we can create an instance of this class in another class and use it to access the function.

Calling Methods

A method can be called via its name. This is demonstrated in the example given below:

```
using System;
using System.IO;


namespace MethodApplication {


class NumberChecker {

   public int CompareValues(int x, int y) {
      /* Declaring a local variable */
      int answer;
```

C# Programming

```
    if (x > y)
        answer = x;
    else
        answer = y;

    return answer;
}
static void Main(string[] args) {
        /* defining a local variable */
        int a = 10;
        int b = 20;
        int res;
        NumberChecker n = new NumberChecker();

        //call CompareValues method
        res = n.CompareValues(a, b);
        Console.WriteLine("The largest value is
: {0}", res );
        Console.ReadLine();
    }
  }
}
```

The code returns the following execution:

```
The largest value is : 20
```

See how we created an instance of the class then used this instance to access the method. Our method also expected two numbers to be passed to it as arguments. That is exactly what we have done as we have passed the numbers 10 and 20 to the function. It compared the two values and returned the largest of them, which is 20.

It is possible for us to call a method from another class. We only have to create an instance of the class in which the method has been defined then use it to access the method. For example, our method *ComapreValues()* has been defined in the *NumberChecker* class. We can create another class, say *MethodChecker* and call the method from there. Let us demonstrate this using a code:

```
using System;
using System.IO;


namespace MethodApplication {


class NumberChecker {


   public int CompareValues(int x, int y) {
      /* Declaring a local variable */
      int answer;


      if (x > y)
         answer = x;
```

```
        else
            answer = y;

        return answer;
    }
}


class MethodChecker {
    static void Main(string[] args) {
        /* defining a local variable */
        int a = 10;
        int b = 20;
        int res;
        NumberChecker n = new NumberChecker();

        //calling the CompareValues method
        res = n.CompareValues(a, b);
        Console.WriteLine("The largest value is
: {0}", res );
        Console.ReadLine();

    }
    }
}
```

The code returns the following when executed:

```
The largest value is : 20
```

We created the *MethodChecker* class. Inside this class, we created an instance of the *NumberChecker* class and gave it the name *n*. We have then used this instance to access this method from the *NumberChecker* class. This shows how powerful an instance of a class. It inherits all the methods and properties of the class.

Recursive Method Call

It is possible for a method to call itself. This process is referred to as *recursion*. Consider the factorial example given below:

```
using System;


namespace MethodApplication {
    class NumberChecker {
        public int factorial(int x) {
            /* declaring a local variable */
            int answer;
            if (x == 1) {
            return 1;
            } else {
                answer = factorial(x - 1) * x;
                return answer;
            }
        }
        static void Main(string[] args) {
```

C# Programming

```
        NumberChecker n = new NumberChecker();
        //let's now call the factorial method
{0}", n.factorial(6));
        Console.WriteLine("Factorial of 6 is :
{0}", n.factorial(6));
        Console.WriteLine("Factorial of 7 is :
{0}", n.factorial(7));
        Console.ReadLine();
    }
  }
}
```

We have created the factorial function and instance of the class named *n*. The code will return the result given below:

```
Factorial of 6 is : 720
Factorial of 7 is : 5040
```

The code was able to give us the factorial of 6 and 7. Note that the factorial of a number of the multiplication of all the numbers below it except 0. For example, the factorial of 6 is 1 * 2 * 3 * 4 * 5 * 6, which gives 720 as shown in the above result.

Passing Parameters to Methods

If a method was defined with parameters, then parameters should be passed to it during the call. We can use any of the three methods for passing parameters to methods. Let us discuss these methods.

C# Programming

Pass By Value

This method involves copying the actual value of an argument to the formal function parameter. This is the default mechanism of passing parameters to a method. With this mechanism, when calling a function, a new location is created in the memory for every value parameter. The values for the actual parameters are then copied into them. This means that the changes that are made to parameter inside the method will have no effect to the argument.

Let us demonstrate this by an example:

```
using System;
```

```
namespace MethodApplication {
    class NumberChecker {
        public void swap(int a, int b) {
            int temp;

            temp = a; /* saving the value of a */
            a = b;     /* putting b into a */
            b = temp; /* putting temp into b */
        }
        static void Main(string[] args) {
            NumberChecker n = new NumberChecker();

            /* defining a local variable */
```

```
            int x = 10;
            int y = 20;


        Console.WriteLine("Before swapping,
value of x is : {0}", x);
        Console.WriteLine("Before swapping,
value of y is : {0}", y);


        /* let's swap the values by calling the
function */
        n.swap(x, y);


        Console.WriteLine("After swapping,
value of x is : {0}", x);
        Console.WriteLine("After swapping,
value of y is : {0}", y);


        Console.ReadLine();
    }
  }
}
```

The code gives the following output:

```
Before swapping, value of x is : 10
Before swapping, value of y is : 20
After swapping, value of x is : 10
After swapping, value of y is : 20
```

What we did is that we changed the values within the function. However, the above output shows that this change did not take effect; hence it has not been reflected above.

That is how we pass parameters by value in C#.

Pass By Reference

A reference parameter references a memory location of a variable. When parameters are passed by reference, no creation of a new memory location, unlike what happens in the pass by value. Reference parameters actually reference the same memory location as the actual parameters being supplied to the method.

To declare reference parameters, we use the *ref* keyword. Let us demonstrate this using an example:

```
using System;

namespace MethodApplication {
    class NumberChecker {
        public void swap(ref int a, ref int b) {
            int temp;

            temp = a; /* saving the value of a */
            a = b;    /* putting b into a */
            b = temp; /* putting temp into b */
        }
```

```
        static void Main(string[] args) {
            NumberChecker n = new NumberChecker();

            /* defining a local variable */
            int x = 10;
            int y = 20;

            Console.WriteLine("Before swapping,
value of x is : {0}", x);
            Console.WriteLine("Before swapping,
value of y is : {0}", y);

            /* let's swap the values by calling the
function */
            n.swap(ref x, ref y);

            Console.WriteLine("After swapping,
value of x is : {0}", x);
            Console.WriteLine("After swapping,
value of y is : {0}", y);

            Console.ReadLine();
        }
    }
}
```

The code returns the following:

C# Programming

```
Before swapping, value of x is : 10
Before swapping, value of y is : 20
After swapping, value of x is : 20
After swapping, value of y is : 10
```

In the pass by value, the values were not swapped. However, in this case, the values have been swapped as shown above. The above change is a reflection is reflected in the *Main* function.

Pass By Output

A return statement can help us to return a single value only from a function. However, by use of *output parameters*, it is possible for on to return two values from a function. Output parameters are the same as reference parameters, with the difference being that they transfer data out of the method instead of into it.

Here is an example demonstrating this:

```
using System;


namespace MethodApplication {
    class NumberChecker {
        public void getValue(out int a ) {
            int temp = 20;
            a = temp;
        }
        static void Main(string[] args) {
            NumberChecker n = new NumberChecker();
```

```
          /* defining a local variable */
          int x = 10;


          Console.WriteLine("Before calling the
method, value of x : {0}", x);


          /* call the function to get value */
          n.getValue(out x);


          Console.WriteLine("After calling the
method, the of value of x is : {0}", x);
          Console.ReadLine();
      }
  }
}
```

It returns the following:

```
Before calling the method, value of x : 10
After calling the method, the of value of x is : 20
```

The variable that is supplied for the output parameter should be assigned a value. Output parameters are very useful when one wants to return values from a method via the parameters without assigning initial value to the parameter. The following example will help you understand this better:

```
using System;
```

```
namespace MethodApplication {
    class NumberChecker {
        public void getValues(out int a, out int b
) {
            Console.WriteLine("Enter in your first
value: ");
            a =
Convert.ToInt32(Console.ReadLine());

            Console.WriteLine("Enter in your
second value: ");
            b =
Convert.ToInt32(Console.ReadLine());
        }
        static void Main(string[] args) {
            NumberChecker n = new NumberChecker();

            /* defining a local variable */
            int x , y;

            /* call a function to obtain the values
*/
            n.getValues(out x, out y);

            Console.WriteLine("After calling the
method, the value of x is : {0}", x);
```

```
        Console.WriteLine("After calling the
method, the value of y is : {0}", y);
        Console.ReadLine();
    }
  }
}
```

You will be prompted to enter the two values, so do those. You will then be provided with their values before and after calling the method.

C# Programming

Chapter 9- Arrays

An array is a special data type that stores a fixed number of values in a sequential manner and by use of a special syntax. All the array elements must belong to the same data type such as a string, integer, double etc. An array can be thought of as a collection of variables of the same type stored in contiguous memory locations. To access a specific element in an array, you use an index.

In the memory, the lowest address identifies the first element in the array while the highest address identifies the highest element in the array.

Declaring Arrays

The declaration of arrays in C# is done using the following syntax:

datatype[] arrayName;

The *datatype* helps us specify the data type of the elements that are stored in the array, not forgetting that all the array elements must belong to the same data type. The square brackets [] help in stating the rank of the array, where the rank denotes the size or the number of elements to be stored in the array. The *arrayName* denotes the name of the array. The following are valid examples of array declarations:

C# Programming

```
int[] intArray;   // may be used for storing int
values
```

```
bool[] boolArray; // may be used for storing
boolean values
```

```
string[] stringArray; // may be used for storing
string values
```

```
double[] doubleArray; // may be used for storing
double values
```

```
byte[] byteArray; // may be used for storing
byte values
```

```
Employee[] customDepartmentArray; // may be used
for storing instances of Employee class
```

Array Initialization

When an array has been declared, it doesn't mean that it has already been initialized in the memory. After initializing an array, it is possible to assign values to it.

The initialization of an array can be done at the time of its declaration using the *new* keyword. When this keyword is used, an instance of the array is created. This is demonstrated below:

C# Programming

```csharp
public class MyArray
{
    public static void Main()
    {
        int[] intArray_1 = new int[4];

        int[] intArray_2 = new int[4]{10, 20, 30, 40};

        int[] intArray_3 = {10, 20, 30, 40};
    }
}
```

First, we have declared an array to store 4 integers. Note that the specification of the array size has been done within the square brackets. We have also done the same thing in our second statement, but values have also been assigned to the indices within the curly braces {}. In the third statement, we have declared an array and assigned values to it without specifying its size.

Late Initialization

It is possible for us to initialize an array after it has been declared. This means that it is not a must for us to do both the declaration and the initialization of an array at the same time. Here is an example:

```csharp
using System;
```

C# Programming

```
public class MyArray
{
        public static void Main()
        {
                string[] array1, array2;

                array1 = new string[4]{ "Nicholas",
                                        "Michelle",
                                        "John",
"Claire",
                                                    };

                array2 = new string[]{"Nicholas",
                                        "Michelle",
                                        "John",
"Claire",
                                            };
                Console.WriteLine(array1.Length);
                Console.WriteLine(array2.Length);
        }
}
```

The above mechanism is known as *late initialization*. The initialization in this case must be done using the *new* keyword. We cannot initialize

C# Programming

the array by simply assigning values to it. The following example shows an invalid initialization of an array:

```
string[] myarray;

myrray = {"Nicholas", "Michelle", "John", "Claire"};
```

Accessing Array Elements

The elements of an array were assigned during the initialization time. However, it is possible for us to assign values to an array using the individual indexes. This is demonstrated below:

```
using System;
public class MyProgram
{
        public static void Main()
        {
                int[] array1 = new int[5];

                array1[0] = 1;

                array1[1] = 2;

                array1[2] = 3;
```

```
        array1[3] = 4;
        array1[4] = 5;
        Console.WriteLine(array1[0]);
        Console.WriteLine(array1[1]);
        Console.WriteLine(array1[2]);
        Console.WriteLine(array1[3]);
        Console.WriteLine(array1[4]);
    }
}
```

The code will return the following result:

```
1
2
3
4
5
```

The retrieval or access to the array values is also done using the indexes. The index of the element is passed within brackets. Consider the example given below:

```
array1[0];
array1[1];
array1[2];
array1[3];
array1[4];
```

C# Programming

That is how we can access all the elements of the above array named *array1*.

Using *for* Loop

We can use a *for* loop to access the elements of an array. The loop will iterate through the elements of the array while accessing the required ones via their indices. For example:

```csharp
using System;
namespace ArrayApp {
   class MyArray {
      static void Main(string[] args) {
         int [] n = new int[10]; /* n is an array of 10 integers */
         int x, y;
         /* initialize the elements of the array n */
         for ( x = 0; x < 10; x++ ) {
            n[ x ] = x + 50;
         }
         /* output each array element's value */
         for (y = 0; y < 10; y++ ) {
            Console.WriteLine("Element at index[{0}] = {1}", y, n[y]);
         }
         Console.ReadKey();
```

C# Programming

```
        }
    }
}
```

The *for* loop for the variable *x* helped us fill 10 values into the array, with the first element being 50 and the last one being 59. The *for* loop for variable y helped us access all the elements of the array right from index 0 to the last index. The output from the program is given below:

```
Element at index[0] = 50
Element at index[1] = 51
Element at index[2] = 52
Element at index[3] = 53
Element at index[4] = 54
Element at index[5] = 55
Element at index[6] = 56
Element at index[7] = 57
Element at index[8] = 58
Element at index[9] = 59
```

Using *foreach* Loop

You have known how to use a *for* loop to access all the elements of an array. A *foreach* loop can also help you to iterate through the elements of an array. The following example demonstrates how to use a *foreach* loop to iterate through the elements of an array:

```
using System;
namespace ArrayApp {
```

C# Programming

```
class MyArray {
    static void Main(string[] args) {
        int [] n = new int[10]; /* n is an array of 10 integers */
        //int x, y;
        /* initialize the elements of the array n */
        for (int x = 0; x < 10; x++ ) {
            n[ x ] = x + 100;
        }
        /* output the values of all array elements */
        foreach (int y in n ) {
            int x = y-100;
            Console.WriteLine("Element[{0}] = {1}", x, y);
        }
        Console.ReadKey();
    }
}
```

The code gives the following result:

The *for* loop helped us fill 10 values into the array, with the first element being 100 and the last one being 109. The *foreach* loop helped us access all the elements of the array right from index 0 to the last index. Note that the variable *x* has been used for filling the array

C# Programming

values while the variable *y* has been used for iterating through the elements of the array. The code returns the output given below:

```
Element[0] = 100
Element[1] = 101
Element[2] = 102
Element[3] = 103
Element[4] = 104
Element[5] = 105
Element[6] = 106
Element[7] = 107
Element[8] = 108
Element[9] = 109
```

Multi-Dimensional Arrays

The concept of multi-dimensional arrays is supported in C#. Such arrays are also known as rectangular arrays. A multi-dimensional arrays is a two dimensional series organized in the form of rows and columns. The following is an example of a multi-dimensional array:

```
int[,] array1 = new int[3,2]{
                            {1, 5},
                            {2, 5},
                            {5, 7}
                    };

// or
int[,] array1 = { {1, 5}, {2, 5}, {5, 7} };
```

As you can see in the above example, to initialize a multi-dimensional array, you must define it in terms of the number of rows and the number of columns. The [3,2] means that the array will have 3 rows and 2 columns.

To access the elements of a multi-dimensional array, we use two indexes. The first index identifies the row while the second one identifies the column. Note that both indexes begin from 0. Let us demonstrate this using an example:

```csharp
using System;
public class MyArray
{
    public static void Main()
    {
        int[,] array1 = new int[3,2]{
                {1, 5},
                {2, 5},
                {5, 7}

        };

        Console.WriteLine(array1[0, 0]);

        Console.WriteLine(array1[0, 1]);
```

```
                    Console.WriteLine(array1[1, 0]);

                    Console.WriteLine(array1[1, 1]);

                    Console.WriteLine(array1[2, 0]);

                    Console.WriteLine(array1[2, 1]);
        }
}
```

The code gives us the following output:

```
1
5
2
5
5
7
```

That is how we can access the elements. The *array1 [2,1]* returns the element located at row 2 and column 1 of the array.

Jagged Arrays

A jagged array is simply an array of arrays. These arrays are storing arrays instead of data type values directly. To initialize a jagged array, we use two square brackets [][]. In the first bracket, we specify the size of the array while in the second bracket, we specify the dimension of the array which is to be stored as values. The following example demonstrates how to declare and initialize a jagged array:

```
using System;
public class MyArray
{
        public static void Main()
        {
                int[][] jaggedArray = new int[2][];

                jaggedArray[0] = new int[4]{1, 2, 3, 4};

                jaggedArray[1] = new int[3]{5, 6, 7};

                Console.WriteLine(jaggedArray[0][0]);

                Console.WriteLine(jaggedArray[0][2]);

                Console.WriteLine(jaggedArray[1][1]);
        }
}
```

C# Programming

We have declared and initialized out jagged array in the above code. The code will give you the following result:

```
1
3
6
```

A jagged array can also store a multi-dimensional array as a value. We can use [,] in the second bracket to indicate a multi-dimension. Here is an example:

```
using System;
public class MyArray
{
        public static void Main()
        {
                int[][,] jaggedArray = new
int[3][,];

                jaggedArray[0] = new int[3, 2] { {
1, 5 }, { 2, 6 }, { 4, 8 } };
                jaggedArray[1] = new int[2, 2] { {
3, 5 }, { 4, 6 } };
                jaggedArray[2] = new int[2, 2];


        Console.WriteLine(jaggedArray[0][1,1]);
```

```
        Console.WriteLine(jaggedArray[1][1,0]);


        Console.WriteLine(jaggedArray[1][1,1]);
    }
}
```

The code will return the following:

```
6
4
6
```

In case an additional bracket is added, then this will become an array of array of array. This is demonstrated in the following example:

```
using System;
public class MyArray
{
        public static void Main()
        {
                int[][][] jaggedArray = new
int[2][][]
                {
                        new int[2][]
                        {
                                new int[3] { 2, 3, 5},
                                new int[2] { 1, 5}
```

C# Programming

```
            },
            new int[1][]
            {
                new int[3] { 7, 6, 8}
            }
        };


        Console.WriteLine(jaggedArray[0][0][0]);


        Console.WriteLine(jaggedArray[0][1][1]);


        Console.WriteLine(jaggedArray[1][0][2]);
    }
}
```

The code returns the following:

```
2
5
8
```

Note that we have used three square brackets [][][], which means an array of array of array. The *jaggedArray* will have 2 elements, which are 2 arrays. Each of these arrays will also have a single dimension array.

Chapter 10- Classes

A class can be seen as a blueprint for an object. Objects in the real world have characteristics like shape, color and functionalities. For example, X6 is an object of car type. A car has characteristics like color, speed, interior, shape etc. This means that any company that creates an object with the above characteristics will be of type car. This means that the Car is a class while each object, that is, a physical car, will be an object of type Car.

In object oriented programming (not forgetting that C# is an object oriented programming language) a class has fields, properties, methods, events etc. A class should define the types of data and the functionality that the objects should have.

With a class, you can create your own custom types by grouping variables of other types together as well as methods and events.

In C#, we use the *class* keyword to define a class. Here is a simple example of this:

```
public class TestClass
{
    public string  field1 = string.Empty;
```

C# Programming

```csharp
    public TestClass()
    {
    }
    public void TestMethod(int param1, string
param2)
    {
        Console.WriteLine("The first parameter
is {0}, and second parameter is {1}",

param1, param2);
    }
    public int AutoImplementedPropertyTest {
get; set; }
    private int propertyVar;
    public int PropertyTest
    {
        get { return propertyVar; }
        set { propertyVar = value; }
    }
}
```

The *public* keyword before the class is an Access Specifier, specifying how the class will be accessed. By being public, it means that it will be accessible by all other classes within the same project. We have given the class the name *TestClass*.

We have also defined a field in the class named *field1*. Below this, we have created a constructor for the class. Note that the constructor

C# Programming

takes the same name as the class itself, hence the constructor's name is *TestClass()*. Inside this class, we have also defined a method named *TestMethod()*, and this method takes in two parameters, *param1* and *param2*, with the former being an integer and the latter being a string.

Here is another example demonstrating how to declare and use a class:

```
using System;
namespace CubeApplication {
    class Cube {
        public double length;   // Length of the cube
        public double breadth;  // Breadth of the cube
        public double height;   // Height of the cube
    }
    class Cubetester {
        static void Main(string[] args) {
            Cube Cube1 = new Cube();   // Declare Cube1 of type Cube
            Cube Cube2 = new Cube();   // Declare Cube2 of type Cube
            double volume = 0.0;   // Store the cube volume here
            // cube 1 specification
```

```
        Cube1.height = 4.0;
        Cube1.length = 5.0;
        Cube1.breadth = 8.0;
        // cube 2 specification
        Cube2.height = 8.0;
        Cube2.length = 12.0;
        Cube2.breadth = 14.0;
        // volume of cube 1
        volume = Cube1.height * Cube1.length *
Cube1.breadth;
        Console.WriteLine("Volume of Cube1 :
{0}", volume);
        // volume of cube 2
        volume = Cube2.height * Cube2.length *
Cube2.breadth;
        Console.WriteLine("Volume of Cube2 :
{0}", volume);
        Console.ReadKey();
    }
  }
}
```

The code will return the following result:

```
Volume of Cube1 : 160
Volume of Cube2 : 1344
```

C# Programming

Encapsulation and Member Functions

A member function for a class is simply a function with a definition or prototype within the definition of the class in the same way as any other function. Such a function can operate on any object of the class in which it is a member, and it can access all the class members for the object.

Member functions are simply the attributes of the object (from a design perspective) and they are defined as *private* so as to implement the concept of encapsulation. We can only access such variables using pubic member functions. Let us demonstrate how we can set and access the various members of a class in C#:

```
using System;
namespace CubeApplication {
   class Cube {
      private double length;    // Length of a
cube
      private double breadth;   // Breadth of a
cube
      private double height;    // Height of a
cube
      public void setLength( double len ) {
         length = len;
      }
```

C# Programming

```csharp
    public void setBreadth( double brea ) {
        breadth = brea;
    }
    public void setHeight( double heig ) {
        height = heig;
    }
    public double getVolume() {
        return length * breadth * height;
    }
}
class Cubetester {
    static void Main(string[] args) {
        Cube Cube1 = new Cube();    // Declare
Cube1 of type Cube
        Cube Cube2 = new Cube();
        double volume;

        // Declare Cube2 of type Cube
        // cube 1 specification
        Cube1.setLength(4.0);
        Cube1.setBreadth(6.0);
        Cube1.setHeight(8.0);

        // cube 2 specification
        Cube2.setLength(10.0);
        Cube2.setBreadth(14.0);
```

```
Cube2.setHeight(12.0);
// volume of cube 1
volume = Cube1.getVolume();
Console.WriteLine("Volume of Cube1 is:
{0}" ,volume);


// volume of cube 2
volume = Cube2.getVolume();
Console.WriteLine("Volume of Cube2 is:
{0}", volume);
Console.ReadKey();
}
}
}
```

Here is the output from the code:

```
Volume of Cube1 is: 192
Volume of Cube2 is: 1680
```

We used the *setter* methods to set the values of the various attributes of our two cubes. The *getVolume()* function has been called to calculate the volumes of the two cubes.

Constructors

A constructor is simply a special member function of a class that is run anytime that we create new objects of the class. A constructor takes the same name as the class and it should not have a return type. The following example demonstrates how to use a constructor in C#:

```csharp
using System;
namespace ConstructorApplication {
    class Person {
        private double height;    // height of the person

        public Person() {
            Console.WriteLine("We are creating an object");
        }
        public void setHeight( double heig ) {
            height = heig;
        }
        public double getHeight() {
            return height;
        }
        static void Main(string[] args) {
            Person p = new Person();
            // set the person's height
            p.setHeight(7.0);
            Console.WriteLine("The height of the person is: {0}", p.getHeight());
            Console.ReadKey();
        }
```

```
        }
}
```

The code should return the following:

```
We are creating an object
The height of the person is: 7
```

A default constructor has no parameters, but it is possible for us to add parameters to a constructor. Such a constructor is known as a *parameterized constructor*. With such a technique, it is possible for one to assign an initial value to an object during the time of its creation. Here is an example:

```csharp
using System;
namespace ConstructorApplication {
    class Person {
        private double height;    // Height of the person
        public Person(double heig) {    // A parameterized constructor
            Console.WriteLine("We are creating an object, height = {0}", heig);
            height = heig;
        }
    public void setHeight( double heig ) {
        height = heig;
    }
```

C# Programming

```
    public double getHeight() {
        return height;
    }
    static void Main(string[] args) {
        Person p = new Person(8.0);
        Console.WriteLine("The height of the
person is : {0}", p.getHeight());
        // set the height
        p.setHeight(7.0);
        Console.WriteLine("The height of the
person is : {0}", p.getHeight());
        Console.ReadKey();
    }
  }
}
```

Here is the output from the code:

```
We are creating an object, height = 8
The height of the person is : 8
The height of the person is : 7
```

Destructors

A destructor refers to a special member function of a class that is run anytime an object of the class goes out of scope. A destructor takes the same name as a class but it should be preceded by a tilde (~). A destructor cannot take parameters neither can it return a value.

A destructor is a useful tool for releasing the memory resources before leaving a program. You can overload or inherit a destructor. The following example demonstrates how to use a destructor:

```
using System;
namespace ConstructorApplication {
  class Person {
    private double height;    // Height of a
person

    public Person() {    // A constructor
      Console.WriteLine("We are creating an
object");
    }
    ~Person() {    //A destructor
      Console.WriteLine("We are deleting an
object");
    }
    public void setHeight( double heig ) {
      height = heig;
    }
    public double getHeight() {
      return height;
    }
    static void Main(string[] args) {
      Person p = new Person();
      // set the height of the person
```

C# Programming

```
        p.setHeight(7.0);

        Console.WriteLine("The height of the
person is : {0}", p.getHeight());

    }

  }

}
```

Here is the output from the function:

```
We are creating an object
The height of the person is : 7
We are deleting an object
```

Static Members

To define a class member as static, we use the *static* keyword. When a class member is declared as static, it means that regardless of the number of objects of the class that are created, there exists only one cope of the static member.

The use of the *static* keyword means that there is only one instance of a member existing in the class. We use this keyword when we need to declare constants since their values can be retrieved by invocation of the class without the creation of an instance of the same. We can initialize static variables outside a class definition or a member function. Static variables can also be initialized inside a class definition.

Let us demonstrate the use of static variables using an example:

```csharp
using System;
namespace StaticApp {
  class StaticVariables {
    public static int x;

    public void count() {
      x++;
    }
    public int getX() {
      return x;
    }
  }
  class StaticTester {
    static void Main(string[] args) {
      StaticVariables var1 = new
StaticVariables();
      StaticVariables var2 = new
StaticVariables();
      var1.count();
      var1.count();
      var1.count();
      var2.count();
      var2.count();
      var2.count();
```

C# Programming

```
        Console.WriteLine("Variable x for var1
is: {0}", var1.getX());
        Console.WriteLine("Variable x for vars
is: {0}", var2.getX());
        Console.ReadKey();
    }
  }
}
```

The code returns the following result:

```
Variable x for var1 is: 6
Variable x for vars is: 6
```

A member function can also declared as static. Such a function will only be able to access static variables. Static functions exist even before the creation of the object. Static functions can be used as demonstrated in the following example:

```
using System;
namespace StaticAppli {
  class StaticVariable {
     public static int x;
     public void count() {
        x++;
     }
     public static int getX() {
        return x;
```

```
        }
    }
    class StaticTester {
        static void Main(string[] args) {
            StaticVariable var = new
StaticVariable();

            var.count();
            var.count();
            var.count();
            Console.WriteLine("Variable x is: {0}",
StaticVariable.getX());
            Console.ReadKey();
        }
    }
}
```

The code will return the following:

```
Variable x is: 3
```

C# Programming

Chapter 11- Structure

A structure in C# is a value type data type. With a structure, you can use a single variable to hold related data belonging to different data types. In C#, we use the *struct* keyword to create a structure.

Structures are used for tracking records. A good example is when you need to keep a record of all class students or all company employees. For the case of storing student records, some of the details that you may need to track including the names, age, course, date of enrollment, date of completion, amount of fee paid, fee balance etc, guardian address and mobile phone number etc. All these details belong to different data types, meaning that you will be required to create a variable for each of them. However, by use of a structure, you can define a single variable and keep these details together as one.

Here is an example of declaring a structure:

```
struct Employee{
    public string name;
    public string department;
    public string title;
    public int age;
    public double salary;
};
```

To initialize a struct, we can choose the *new* keyword or not. The members of a struct can be assigned values as shown below:

```csharp
using System;

public class MyStruct
{
    public static void Main()
    {
    Employee emp = new Employee()
            emp.name = "Nicholas Samuel";
            emp.department = "Computing";
            emp.age = 26;
            emp.salary = 5000;
            Console.WriteLine(emp.name);
        Console.WriteLine(emp.department);
            Console.WriteLine(emp.age);
            Console.WriteLine(emp.salary);


    }
}

public struct Employee
{
        public string name { get; set; }
```

```
    public string department { get; set; }
    public string title { get; set; }
    public int age { get; set; }
    public double salary { get; set; }
}
```

The code gives the following result:

```
Nicholas Samuel
Computing
26
5000
```

The struct named *Employee* was defined using the *struct* keyword. The various details of this struct have been declared within this. At the top of the class, we created an instance of this struct and we gave it the name *emp*. This instance has been used to access the various attributes of the struct for display on the screen.

Note that a struct is a value type, and this makes it faster when compared to a class object. This has made them good for use in game programming. However, one can easily transfer a class object than a struct. This means that a struct should not be used when one is need of transferring data to other classes.

Here is another example of a struct in C#:

```
using System;
```

```csharp
struct Cars {
    public string model;
    public int cc;
    public int passengers;
    public int year;
};
public class carStructure {
    public static void Main(string[] args) {
        Cars Premio;    /* Declare prenio of type Car */
        Cars X6;    /* Declare X6 of type Car */
        /* premio specification */
        Premio.model = "Saloon";
        Premio.cc = 1800;
        Premio.passengers = 5;
        Premio.year = 2010;
        /* X6 specification */
        X6.model = "Saloon";
        X6.cc = 3500;
        X6.passengers = 5;
        X6.year = 2012;
        /* print premio info */
        Console.WriteLine( "Premio model: {0}",
Premio.model);
        Console.WriteLine("Premio CC : {0}",
Premio.cc);
```

```
    Console.WriteLine("Premio passengers :
{0}", Premio.passengers);

    Console.WriteLine("Premio year :{0}",
Premio.year);

    /* print X6 info */

    Console.WriteLine( "X6 model: {0}",
X6.model);

    Console.WriteLine("X6 CC : {0}", X6.cc);

    Console.WriteLine("X6 passengers : {0}",
X6.passengers);

    Console.WriteLine("X6 year :{0}",
X6.year);

    Console.ReadKey();

  }

}
```

The code will return the following details:

```
Premio model: Saloon
Premio CC : 1800
Premio passengers : 5
Premio year :2010
X6 model: Saloon
X6 CC : 3500
X6 passengers : 5
X6 year :2012
```

We have created a single struct named *Cars*. In this structure, we have stored the two members, Premio and X6. These two instances are instances of the structure. The properties for these had been defined inside the structure. The two instances share properties, but these will take different values. We have then printed the values of these properties as shown in the above output.

Characteristics of Structures

So far, you have known how to use structures and some of their characteristics. The structures in C# have a great difference from the structures supported in C and C++. C# structures have the features described below:

- Structures may have fields, indexers, methods, properties, operators and events.

- A structure can have defined constructors, not destructors. However, in a structure, we are not allowed to define a default constructor. The reason is that this is defined automatically and one cannot change it.

- A structure cannot inherit another structure or a class.

- With a structure, we can implement one or more interfaces.

- The members of a structure cannot be specified as virtual abstract or protected.

- After the creation of a Struct object via the *New* keyword, the struct object is created and the necessary constructor is called. Unlike classes, we can instantiate a struct without the use of the *New* keyword.

- If we don't use the New operator, the fields will not be assigned and it will not be possible to use the object until an assignment has been done to all the fields.

Struct vs. Class

Here the differences between Structs and Classes:

- Structs are value types while classes are reference types.

- Structs don't support inheritance. Classes do.

- A Struct cannot have a default constructor. A class can have.

Let us create an example in relation to the above differences:

```
using System;
struct Cars {
    private string model;
    private int cc;
    private int passengers;
    private int year;
```

C# Programming

```
    public void getValues(string m, int c, int p,
int yr) {
        model = m;
        cc = c;
        passengers = p;
        year = yr;
    }
    public void show() {
        Console.WriteLine("Car model : {0}",
model);
        Console.WriteLine("CC : {0}", cc);
        Console.WriteLine("Passengers : {0}",
passengers);
        Console.WriteLine("Year :{0}", year);
    }
};
public class myStructure {
    public static void Main(string[] args) {
        Cars Premio = new Cars();   /* Declare
Premio of type Cars */
        Cars X6 = new Cars();    /* Declare X6 of
type Cars */
        /* Premio specification */
        Premio.getValues("Saloon",
        1800, 5, 2012);
        /* X6 specification */
        X6.getValues("Saloon",
```

```
        3500, 5, 2012);
        /* print Premio info */
        Premio.show();
        /* print X6 info */
        X6.show();
        Console.ReadKey();
    }
}
```

The code will give the following output after execution:

```
Car model : Saloon
CC : 1800
Passengers : 5
Year :2012
Car model : Saloon
CC : 3500
Passengers : 5
Year :2012
```

C# Programming

Chapter 12- Encapsulation

Encapsulation is the process of enclosing items within a logical or physical package. In object oriented programming, encapsulation is used to prevent access to the implementation details.

Encapsulation and Abstraction are closely related features in object oriented programming. The purpose of abstraction is to make the relevant details visible to users while the purpose of encapsulation is to enable a programmer to implement the required level of abstraction.

To implement encapsulation, we use *access specifiers*. The role of an access specifier is to state the visibility and scope of a class member. There are different types of access specifiers that are supported in C#. They include the following:

- Public

- Protected

- Private

- Protected internal

- Internal

C# Programming

Private Access Specifier

With a private access specifier, a class is able to hide its member functions and member variables from other objects and functions. Only functions of a similar class are able to access its private members. An instance of the class is not able to access the private members of the class. Consider the example given below:

```
using System;
namespace AccessApplication {
    class Figure {
    // The class member variables
        private double width;
        private double length;
    public void GetDetails() {
        Console.WriteLine("Enter the Length:
");
        length =
Convert.ToDouble(Console.ReadLine());
        Console.WriteLine("Enter the Width: ");
        width =
Convert.ToDouble(Console.ReadLine());
    }
    public double CalculateArea() {
        return length * width;
    }
    public void Show() {
```

```
            Console.WriteLine("The Length of the
figure is: {0}", length);
            Console.WriteLine("The Width of the
figure is: {0}", width);
            Console.WriteLine("The Area of the
figure is: {0}", CalculateArea());
        }
    }//end the class Figure
    class RunFigure {
        static void Main(string[] args) {
            Figure f = new Figure();
            f.GetDetails();
            f.Show();
            Console.ReadLine();
        }
    }
}
```

Run the code and enter the measurements of the figure, both the width and the length. You will get the area of the figure.

The member variables, that is, the *width* and the *length* have been defined as *private*. This means that we cannot access them from the Main() function. The *GetDetails()* and *Show()* member functions have been declared as *public*, hence they are able to access these variables. We can also access them from the *Main()* function after creating an instance of the *Figure* class. This instance has been given the name *f*.

C# Programming

Public Access Specifier

With a public access specifier, a class is able to expose its member functions and member variables to the other objects and functions. Any class member declared as public can be accessed from outside of that class. Consider the following example:

```csharp
using System;
namespace FigureApplication {
    class Figure {
        // The class member variables
        public double width;
        public double length;
        public double CalculateArea() {
            return length * width;
        }
        public void Show() {
            Console.WriteLine("The Length of the
figure is: {0}", length);
            Console.WriteLine("The Width of the
figure is: {0}", width);
            Console.WriteLine("The Area of the
figure is: {0}", CalculateArea());
        }
    }//end the Figure class
    class RunFigure {
        static void Main(string[] args) {
```

```
        Figure f = new Figure();
        f.length = 5.4;
        f.width = 3.2;
        f.Show();
        Console.ReadLine();
    }
  }
}
```

The following is the output from the code:

```
The Length of the figure is: 5.4
The Width of the figure is: 3.2
The Area of the figure is: 17.28
```

The class member variables *width* and *length* have been declared as *public*, which means that we are able to access them from the *Main()* function after creating an instance of the class. We have created an instance of the *Figure* class and given it the name *f*.

The *CalculateArea()* and *Show()* member functions are also able to access these member variables without using an instance of the class. The *Show()* member function has also been declared as public, meaning that we are able to access it from the *Main()* function using an instance of the class.

Protected Access Specifier

This type of access specifier makes it possible for a child class to access the member functions and member variables that have been defined in the base class. This way, it becomes possible for us to implement inheritance. This will be discussed in inheritance.

Internal Access Specifier

This type of access specifier allows a class to expose its member functions and member variables to the other objects and functions in the current assembly. This means that any member that has been created using the internal access specifier is accessible from any class or method that has been defined within the application where the member has been defined. This is demonstrated in the following example:

```csharp
using System;
namespace AccesserApplication {
   class Figure {
      // The member variables
      internal double width;
      internal double length;
      double CalculateArea() {
         return length * width;
      }
```

```csharp
    public void Show() {
        Console.WriteLine("The Length of the
figure is: {0}", length);
        Console.WriteLine("The Width of the
figure is: {0}", width);
        Console.WriteLine("The Area of the
figure is: {0}", CalculateArea());
    }
}//end the class Figure


class RunFigure {
    static void Main(string[] args) {
        Figure f = new Figure();
        f.length = 6.5;
        f.width = 4.8;
        f.Show();
        Console.ReadLine();
    }
}
}
```

The code should return the following result:

```
The Length of the figure is: 6.5
The Width of the figure is: 4.8
The Area of the figure is: 31.2
```

C# Programming

Chapter 13- Inheritance

Inheritance is a very important feature in object oriented programming. With inheritance, it is possible for a programmer to define one class in terms of another class. This also makes it possible for us to reuse code and shorten the time taken to implement an application.

During the creation of a class, instead of having to create completely new member functions and data members, the programmer is able to designate that the new class inherits the members of an already existing class. The already existing class is known as the *base class* while the new class is known as the *derived class*.

Inheritance is simply an implementation of IS-A relationship. For example, Cow is a Mammal.

It is possible for a class to inherit from more than one class or interfaces, meaning that it can inherit data and functions from many base interfaces or classes. The following example demonstrates the concept of the base and derived class:

```
using System;
namespace InheritanceApp {
    class Figure {
```

```
    public void setWidth(int wid) {
        width = wid;
    }
    public void setHeight(int heig) {
        height = heig;
    }
    protected int width;
    protected int height;
}
// A Derived class
class Rectangle: Figure {
    public int calculateArea() {
        return (width * height);
    }
}
class TestInheritance {
    static void Main(string[] args) {
        Rectangle R = new Rectangle();
        R.setWidth(6);
        R.setHeight(8);
        // Print the rectangle's area.
        Console.WriteLine("The area is: {0}",
R.calculateArea());
        Console.ReadKey();
    }
}
```

}

The code should return the following output:

```
The area is: 48
```

We have defined the *Figure* class with two properties namely *width* and *height*. This class also has two methods, *setWidth()* and *SetHeight()*. We have then defined a class named *Rectangle*. Notice the syntax we have used to create this class:

```
class Rectangle: Figure {
```

The use of the full colon signals that the Rectangle class is inheriting the Figure class. The Rectangle class only has one method, the *calculateArea()* method. However, since it has inherited the Figure class, it means that it has all the properties of the Figure class, like the width and the height.

We have then created the *TestInheritance* class. Within the Main() method, we have created an instance of the Rectangle class and given it the name R. We have used this instance to access the properties that have been defined in both the Rectangle and the Figure classes. That is how powerful inheritance is!

C# Programming

Base Class Initialization

The derived class inherits the member methods and member variables defined in the base class. This means that we should create the super class object before creating the subclass. Instructions for initialization of the superclass can be given in the initialization of the list of members.

This is demonstrated in the program given below:

```
using System;
namespace InheritanceApp {
   class Object {
      // The member variables
      protected double width;
      protected double length;
      public Object(double len, double wid) {
          width = wid;
          length = len;
      }
      public double CalculateArea() {
          return length * width;
      }
      public void Show() {
          Console.WriteLine("The Width of the
figure is: {0}", width);
```

```csharp
        Console.WriteLine("The Length of the
figure is: {0}", length);
        Console.WriteLine("The Area of the
figure is: {0}", CalculateArea());
    }
  }//end class Figure
  class Carpet : Object {
    private double cost;
    public Carpet(double len, double wid) :
base(len, wid) { }
    public double CalculateCost() {
      double cost;
      cost = CalculateArea() * 120;
      return cost;
    }
    public void Show() {
      base.Show();
      Console.WriteLine("The toatl cost for
the caprpet is: {0}", CalculateCost());
    }
  }
  class RunObject {
    static void Main(string[] args) {
      Carpet c = new Carpet(7.5, 9.5);
      c.Show();
      Console.ReadLine();
    }
```

C# Programming

```
    }
}
```

The code will return the following output:

```
The Width of the figure is: 9.5
The Length of the figure is: 7.5
The Area of the figure is: 71.25
The toatl cost for the caprpet is: 8550
```

Multiple Inheritance

Multiple inheritance is not supported in C#. However, with interfaces, it is possible for us to implement multiple inheritance. Consider the following example:

```
using System;
namespace InheritanceApp {
    class Object {
        public void setWidth(int wid) {
            width = wid;
        }
        public void setHeight(int heig) {
            height = heig;
        }
        protected int width;
        protected int height;
    }
```

```csharp
// PaintCost for the Base class
public interface PaintCost {
    int calculateCost(int area);
}
// The derived class
class Board : Object, PaintCost {
    public int calculateArea() {
        return (width * height);
    }
    public int calculateCost(int area) {
        return area * 120;
    }
}
class InheritanceTester {
    static void Main(string[] args) {
        Board B = new Board();
        int area;
        B.setWidth(5);
        B.setHeight(7);
        area = B.calculateArea();
        // Show the area of the object
        Console.WriteLine("The area of the
object is: {0}",  B.calculateArea());
        Console.WriteLine("The toal printing
cost is: ${0}" , B.calculateCost(area));
```

C# Programming

```
        Console.ReadKey();
    }
  }
}
```

The code gives the following output:

```
The area of the object is: 35
The toal printing cost is: $4200
```

Chapter 14- Polymorphism

Polymorphism is a term that means taking many forms. In programming, it is expressed as **"one interface, many functions"**. Polymorphism can take two forms, static or dynamic.

For the case of static dynamism, response to the function is determined during compile time. In dynamic polymorphism, response to the function is determined during runtime.

Static Polymorphism

As stated above, the response to a function in this type of polymorphism is determined during compile time. The process of linking a function to an object during compile time is known as *early binding*. It is also known as *static binding*. In C#, static polymorphism can be implemented in two ways:

- Function overloading
- Operator overloading

Function Overloading

It is possible for us to have multiple definitions for the same function name within one scope. The differences between these functions are implemented by types or the number of arguments that the functions

C# Programming

take. Function declarations cannot be overloaded by differing the return types only.

The following example demonstrates how to overload a function in C#:

```csharp
using System;

namespace PolymorphismApp {
  class DisplayData {
    void display(int x) {
      Console.WriteLine("Printing an int value: {0}", x );
    }
    void display(double y) {
      Console.WriteLine("Printing a float value: {0}" , y);
    }
    void display(string z) {
      Console.WriteLine("Printing a string value: {0}", z);
    }
    static void Main(string[] args) {
      DisplayData dd = new DisplayData();

      // Call display function to return an integer value
      dd.display(10);
```

```
        // Call display function to return a
float value
        dd.display(11.385);
        // Call display function to return a
string value
        dd.display("Hello Sir/Madam");
        Console.ReadKey();
    }
  }
}
```

The code will return the following once executed:

```
Printing an int value: 10
Printing a float value: 11.385
Printing a string value: Hello Sir/Madam
```

We have three definitions of the function *display()*. In this case, overloading has been implementing by varying the types of parameters taken by the function. In one instance, the function is taking an integer value, a float in another instance and a string in the last instance.

Operator Overloading

Operator overloading refers to the use of a single operator to perform various operations. With operator overloading, additional functionalities can be added to the C# operators during their application on user-defined types. This is the case when either one or both the operands belong to a user-defined class.

Here is an example that demonstrates this:

```csharp
using System;
namespace PolymorphismApp {
  class Object {
          private double breadth;   // The breadth of the box
          private double length;    // The Length of the box
          private double height;    // The Height of the box
      public double calculateVolume() {
          return breadth * length * height;
      }
      public void setLength( double l ) {
          length = l;
      }
      public void setBreadth( double b ) {
          breadth = b;
      }
      public void setHeight( double h ) {
          height = h;
      }
```

```csharp
    // Overload the + operator to add 2 objects.
    public static Object operator+ (Object obj1, Object obj2) {
        Object ob = new Object();
        ob.length = obj1.length + obj2.length;
        ob.breadth = obj1.breadth + obj2.breadth;
        ob.height = obj1.height + obj2.height;
        return ob;
    }
}
class BoxTester {
    static void Main(string[] args) {
        Object Object1 = new Object();    // Declare Object1 of type Object
        Object Object2 = new Object();    // Declare Object2 of type Object
        Object Object3 = new Object();    // Declare Object3 of type Object
        double volume = 0.0;    // Store volume of the object here
        // object 1 dimensions
        Object1.setLength(7.0);
        Object1.setBreadth(8.0);
        Object1.setHeight(10.0);
        // Object 2 dimensions
        Object2.setLength(6.0);
```

C# Programming

```csharp
        Object2.setBreadth(9.0);
        Object2.setHeight(11.0);


        // Calculate the volume of object 1
        volume = Object1.calculateVolume();
        Console.WriteLine("The volume of
Object1 : {0}", volume);
        // Calculate the volume of object 2
        volume = Object2.calculateVolume();
        Console.WriteLine("The volume of
Object2 : {0}", volume);
        // Add the two objects
        Object3 = Object1 + Object2;
        // Calculate the volume of object 3
        volume = Object3.calculateVolume();
        Console.WriteLine("The volume of
Object3 : {0}", volume);
        Console.ReadKey();
    }
  }
}
```

The code returns the following output:

```
The volume of Object1 : 560
The volume of Object2 : 594
The volume of Object3 : 4641
```

We have overloaded the + operator. The operator is used for addition of two numeric types. However, in the above example, we have used the operator to add the two objects together, that is, Object1 and Object2. This has given us Object3. The Object1 and Object2 are user-defined types, meaning that we have used the + operator to add user-defined types.

Note that it is true that we can overload operators in C#, but not all operators can be overloaded. For example, you cannot overload the comparison operators like ==, <, >, !=, >= and <=. For the case of the conditional logic operators like && and ||, we can overload them, but not directly.

Dynamic Polymorphism

With C#, we can create abstract classes that are good for a partial class implementation of an interface. The completion of this is implemented once after a derived class has inherited from it. An abstract class has abstract methods, and the derived class implements these. However, the derived class a more specialized functionality.

Note that you cannot create an instance of any class that is abstract. An abstract method cannot also be declared outside an abstract class. If a C# class is declared as *sealed*, it means that the class cannot be

inherited. However, you are not allowed to declare an abstract class
sealed. Here is an example of an abstract class:

```csharp
using System;
namespace PolymorphismApp {
    abstract class Object {
        public abstract int area();
    }
    class Object1: Object {
        private int width;
        private int length;
        public Object1( int x = 0, int y = 0) {
            length = x;
            width = y;
        }
        public override int area () {
            Console.WriteLine("The Object1 area
is:");
            return (width * length);
        }
    }
    class Object1Tester {
        static void Main(string[] args) {
            Object1 obj = new Object1(8, 6);
            double x = obj.area();
```

```
        Console.WriteLine("The area is:
{0}",x);

        Console.ReadKey();
    }

  }

}
```

The code will print the following result:

```
The Object1 area is:
The area is: 48
```

After defining a function in a class that you want to implement in an inherited class, you should use a *virtual* function.

To implement dynamic polymorphism, we use *abstract classes* and *virtual functions*. Let us demonstrate this using an example:

```
using System;
namespace PolymorphismApp {
   class Object {
     protected int width, height;
     public Object( int x = 0, int y = 0) {
        width = x;
        height = y;
     }
     public virtual int area() {
```

```
        Console.WriteLine("The area of the
parent class is :");
        return 0;
    }
  }
  class Object1: Object {
    public Object1( int x = 0, int y = 0):
base(x, y) {

    }
    public override int area () {
        Console.WriteLine("The area of Object1
class is:");
        return (width * height);
    }
  }
  class Object2: Object {
    public Object2(int x = 0, int y = 0):
base(x, y) {
    }
    public override int area() {
        Console.WriteLine("The area of Object2
class is:");
        return (width * height / 2);
    }
  }
  class Caller {
```

```
        public void CallArea(Object obj) {
            int x;
            x = obj.area();
            Console.WriteLine("The Area is: {0}",
x);
        }
    }
    class TesterClass {
        static void Main(string[] args) {
            Caller c = new Caller();
            Object1 ob1 = new Object1(10, 7);
            Object2 ob2 = new Object2(10, 5);
            c.CallArea(ob1);
            c.CallArea(ob2);
            Console.ReadKey();
        }
    }
}
```

The code returns the following output:

```
The area of Object1 class is:
The Area is: 70
The area of Object2 class is:
The Area is: 25
```

C# Programming

Chapter 15- Regular Expressions

A regular expression is simply a pattern that we can match against an input text. In the .Net framework, there is a regular expression engine that we can use to perform that matching. A pattern is made up of one or even more operators, character literals or constructs.

Regex Class

This is a class used for representation of regular expressions. This class comes with a number inbuilt function such as the following:

1. public bool isMatch(string input)- the method specifies whether the specified regular expression in the Regex constructor gets a match in the specified input string.

2. public bool isMatch(string input, int startPoint)- the method specifies whether the specified regular expression in the Regex constructor gets a match in the specified input string from the specified location in the input string.

3. public static bool isMatch(string input, int pattern)- the method specifies whether the specified regular expression gets a match in the specified input string.

4.   public MatchCollection Matches(string input, string replacement)- this replaces a match in the input string with the specified replacement string.

5.   public string[] Split(string input)- this function helps in splitting an input string into an array of substrings at positions that have been defined by the regular expression pattern that is specified in a Regex constructor.

Consider the example given below:

```
using System.Text.RegularExpressions;
using System;


namespace RegularExpApp {
  class MyProgram {
      private static void findMatch(string
input, string expre) {
          Console.WriteLine("The Expression is: "
+ expre);
          MatchCollection mc =
Regex.Matches(input, expre);
          foreach (Match x in mc) {
              Console.WriteLine(x);
          }
      }
      static void Main(string[] args) {
```

```
        string s = "Splitting an Input String
into Substrings";


        Console.WriteLine("Match words that
begin with 'S': ");
        findMatch(s, @"\bS\S*");
        Console.ReadKey();
    }
  }
}
```

After the match, the code will return the following:

```
Match words that begin with 'S':
The Expression is: \bS\S*
Splitting
String
Substrings
```

The output shows that three words have been matched from the input string. We were matching any words that begin with S and three of them were found.

Consider the next example given below:

```
using System.Text.RegularExpressions;
using System;
namespace RegularExpApp {
    class MyProgram {
        private static void findMatch(string
input, string expre) {
```

C# Programming

```
        Console.WriteLine("The input expression
is: " + expre);
        MatchCollection mc =
Regex.Matches(input, expre);
        foreach (Match x in mc) {
            Console.WriteLine(x);
        }
    }
    static void Main(string[] args) {
        string s = "so she was the same";


        Console.WriteLine("Match words
beginning with 's' and ending with 'e':");
        findMatch(s, @"\bs\S*e\b");
        Console.ReadKey();
    }
  }
}
```

The code will give the following result:

```
Match words beginning with 's' and ending with 'e':
The input expression is: \bs\S*e\b
she
same
```

In the above example, we are matching the words that begin with s and end with e. We have successfully matched two words in the input string. Here is another example:

```
using System;
using System.Text.RegularExpressions;
namespace RegularExpApp {
    class MyProgram {
        static void Main(string[] args) {
            string text = "Hi    learner    ";
            string pattern = "\\s+";
            string substitute = " ";
            Regex r = new Regex(pattern);
            string output = r.Replace(text, substitute);
            Console.WriteLine("The input string is: {0}", text);
            Console.WriteLine("The string after replacement is: {0}", output);
            Console.ReadKey();
        }
    }
}
```

The code returns the following:

```
The input string is: Hi    learner
The string after replacement is: Hi learner
```

What we are doing in the code is that we are replacing the extra white space. There is a big space between "Hi" and "learner". The extra one has been replaced or removed.

C# Programming

Chapter 16- Handling Exceptions

Applications usually encounter errors during execution. After the occurrence of an error, the program throws an exception with more information regarding the error. Exceptions should be handled to prevent a program from crashing.

In C#, exceptions are handled using 4 main keywords:

1. try- this keyword identifies the block of code in which particular exceptions have been activated. It is then followed by either one or more *catch* blocks.

2. catch- a program should catch an exception with an exception handler at a place within the program where you need to handle the problem. The *catch* is a keyword that indicates a place where the exception will be caught.

3. finally- the finally block is used for executing a set of statements regardless of whether an exception has been thrown or not. For example, a file must be closed after being opened, whether an exception is thrown or not.

C# Programming

4.   throw- an exception is normally thrown after the occurrence of a problem. This is done via the *throw* keyword.

A combination of *try* and *catch* is used for catching exceptions. The try/catch block has to be placed around a code that may raise an exception. Such code is said to be *protected*, and here is the syntax for using these keywords:

```
try {
    // statements raising the exception
} catch( ExceptionName exception1 ) {
    // The error handling code
} catch( ExceptionName exception2 ) {
    // The error handling code
} catch( ExceptionName eexceptionN ) {
    // The error handling code
} finally {
    // statements to execute
}
```

One can use many catch statements with the goal of catching many different exceptions if many exceptions are raised by the *try* block.

In C#, exceptions are represented using classes. The *System.Exception* acts as the base class for all exception classes in C# since all other classes are derived from it, either directly or indirectly.

Handling Exceptions

In C#, exceptions can be handled using the *try* and *catch* blocks. With these blocks, we can separate the core program statements from statements for handing errors. We can handle errors using the *try*, *catch* and *finally* keywords.

A division by zero should for example raise an exception as it not mathematically supported. Let us create some code to handle this:

```csharp
using System;
namespace ExceptionHandlingApp {
    class DivisionClass {
        int answer;
        DivisionClass() {
            answer = 0;
        }
        public void division(int x, int y) {
            try {
                answer = x / y;
            } catch (DivideByZeroException exception) {
                Console.WriteLine("Exception caught: {0}", exception);
            } finally {
                Console.WriteLine("Answer: {0}", answer);
```

```
        }
    }
        static void Main(string[] args) {
            DivisionClass dc = new DivisionClass();
            dc.division(12, 0);
            Console.ReadKey();
        }
    }
}
```

The code should return the exception given below:

```
Exception caught: System.DivideByZeroException: Attempted to divide by
    at ExceptionHandlingApp.DivisionClass.division (System.Int32 x, Syst
Answer: 0
```

We created the *division()* function that takes two arguments, x and y, of type integer. We have then passed 12 and 0 to the function, meaning that we will be dividing 12 by 0. However, this has generated an exception since division by zero is not allowed.

User-Defined Exceptions

C# allows programmers to define their own exceptions. We derive such user-defined exception classes from the *Exception* class. Consider the example given below:

```
using System;
namespace ExceptionHandlingApp {
```

```csharp
class TemperatureTest {
    static void Main(string[] args) {
        TemperatureClass tc = new
TemperatureClass();
        try {
            tc.displayTemperature();
        } catch(TempIsZeroException exception)
{

Console.WriteLine("TempIsZeroException: {0}",
exception.Message);
        }
        Console.ReadKey();
    }
}
public class TempIsZeroException: Exception {
    public TempIsZeroException(string msg):
base(msg) {
    }
}
public class TemperatureClass {
    int temp = 0;

    public void displayTemperature() {

        if(temp == 0) {
```

C# Programming

```
        throw (new TempIsZeroException("We
found Zero Temperature"));
        } else {
        Console.WriteLine("Temperature is:
{0}", temp);
        }
    }
}
```

The code will return the following:

```
TempIsZeroException: We found Zero Temperature
```

Nested try-catch

C# allows us to create a block of nested try-catch. In such a case, the exception will be caught in the catch block following the try block in which the exception occurred. Consider the following example:

```
using System;
public class NestedtryCatch
{
        public static void Main()
        {
                Employee emp = null;

                try
                {
```

```
                    try
                    {
                            emp.EmployeeName = "";
                    }
                    catch
                    {
                        Console.WriteLine("The
inner catch");
                    }
            }
            catch
            {
                Console.WriteLine("The outer
catch");
            }
        }
}


public class Employee{

        public string EmployeeName { get; set; }
}
```

The code prints the following:

```
The inner catch
```

C# Programming

In case there is no inner catch block with the necessary exception type, the exception will flow to outer catch block until an appropriate exception filter is found. Here is an example:

```
using System;
public class NestedtryCatch
{
        public static void Main()
        {
                Employee emp = null;

                try
                {
                        try
                        {
                                // This will throw a
NullReferenceException
                                emp.EmployeeName = "";
                        }
                        catch
(InvalidOperationException innerException)
                        {
                                Console.WriteLine("The
inner catch");
                        }
                }
                catch
```

```
                {
                        Console.WriteLine("The outer
catch");
                }
        }
}


public class Employee{

        public string EmployeeName { get; set; }
}
```

In the example given above, the statement *emp.EmployeeName* will generate a NullReferenceException, but we don't have a catch block that handles a NullReferenceException or an Exception type. The outer block will handle this. The code returns the following:

```
The outer catch
```

C# Programming

Chapter 17- File Input/ Output

A file is characterized by a name and a directory path. Once a file has been opened, it becomes a *stream*. Files are normally opened for reading or writing purposes.

The stream is simply the sequence of bytes that pass through the communication path. Streams are of two types:

- Input stream
- Output stream

The input stream helps us to read data from a file, that is, a read operation, while the output stream helps us to write data into a file, that is, a write operation.

Input/ Output Classes

C# provides us with a number of classes that we can use for working with files. These classes can be used for accessing directories, files, creating new files, opening existing files and moving files from one directory to another. These classes are defined in the System.IO class. Let us discuss some of these classes:

- BinaryReader- this class helps us in reading primitive data from a binary stream.

- BinaryWriter- this class helps us in writing primitive data in a binary format.

- BufferedStream- this acts as a temporary storage for bytes of streams.

- Directory- this class helps us to manipulate the structure of a directory.

- DriveInfo- this class provides us with information about the drives.

- File- this class is used for manipulation of files.

- FileInfo- helps in performing operations on files.

- FileStream- used for writing and reading from any location in a file.

- MemoryStream- helps in randomly accessing data kept in a memory.

- Path- for performing operations on path information.

- StreamReader- reads characters from a stream of bytes.

- StreamWriter- writes characters to a stream.

- StringReader- reads from a string buffer.

- StringWriter- writes into a string buffer.

FileStream Class

This class is defined in the System.IO namespace and it helps us to read from and write to files. We can also use it to close files.

For you to be able to use this class, you have to create its object. This instance can then be used for creating new files and opening existing files. Here is how you can create an instance of the FileStream class:

```
FileStream <object> = new FileStream( <file>,
<FileMode Enumerator>,
    <FileAccess Enumerator>, <FileShare
Enumerator>);
```

For example, suppose we need to read a file names *names.txt*. We can create a FileStream object named *FS* and use it for this purpose. This is demonstrated below:

```
FileStream FS = new FileStream("names.txt",
FileMode.Open, FileAccess.Read, FileShare.Read);
```

The FileMode is an enumerator that defines a number of methods that can be used for opening files. These methods include the following:

C# Programming

- Append – this method opens an existing file then puts the cursor at the end of file, or it creates a new file if the specified file doesn't exist.

- Create – for creating a new file.

- CreateNew – It instructs the operating system to create a new file.

- Open – for opening an existing file.

- OpenOrCreate – It instructs the operating system to open a file if it is in existence or create a new file if it doesn't exist.

- Truncate – for opening an existing file and truncating its size to zero bytes.

The FileAccess is an enumerator that comes with a number of methods including Read, Write and ReadWrite.

The FileShare enumerator comes with the following members:

- Inheritable – helps a file handle in passing inheritance to child processes.

- None – It disables sharing of current file.

- Read – It opens a file for reading.

- ReadWrite – opens a file for reading and writing.

- Write – opens a file for writing.

C# Programming

The FileStream class can be used as demonstrated below:

```
using System.IO;
using System;
namespace FileApp {
    class MyProgram {
        static void Main(string[] args) {
            FileStream FS = new
FileStream("names.dat", FileMode.OpenOrCreate,
                FileAccess.ReadWrite);
            for (int x = 1; x <= 10; x++) {
                FS.WriteByte((byte)x);
            }
            FS.Position = 0;
            for (int x = 0; x <= 10; x++) {
                Console.Write(FS.ReadByte() + " ");
            }
            FS.Close();
            Console.ReadKey();
        }
    }
}
```

The code will return the following output after execution:

```
1 2 3 4 5 6 7 8 9 10 -1
```

C# Programming

Appending Text Lines

Sometimes, you may need to append a number of text lines to a file. This can be done by calling the *AppendAllLines()* method. Here is an example:

```
string multipleLines = "The first line." +
Environment.NewLine +
                       "The second line." +
Environment.NewLine +
                       "The third line.";


// To open the file named Myfile.txt then append
the abovelines. If the file does not exist, a
new one will be created.
File.AppendAllLines(@"C:\MyFile.txt",
multipleLines.Split(Environment.NewLine.ToCharAr
ray()).ToList<string>());
```

The file will be opened and the specified lines will be appended to the file.

Appending a String

The *File.AppendAllText()* method can allow you to append a string to a file in only a single line of code. This is demonstrated below:

```
//Open the file named MyFile.txt then append
text to it. If the file does not exists, create
a new one and open it for writing.
```

```
File.AppendAllText(@"C:\ MyFile.txt", "This
string will be written into the file");
```

Overwriting Text

If you need to overwrite a file, use the *File.WriteAllText()* method. The method will delete the text in the file and replace it with the one that you specify. This method can be used as demonstrated below:

```
// To open  the file MyFile.txt and write the
text into it. If the file does not exit, a new
one will be created and opened for writing.
File.WriteAllText(@"C:\MyFile.txt", "This text
will be used for replacing the current text in
the file.");
```

With the Static File Class, one can perform various operations. This is demonstrated below:

```
//Check whether the file exists  at the
specified location or not
bool isFileExists = File.Exists(@"C:\
MyFile.txt"); // it will return false


//Copy MyFile.txt as the new file MyNewFile.txt
File.Copy(@"C:\MyFile.txt",
@"D:\MyNewFile.txt");


// Check when the file was lastly accessed
DateTime lastAccessTime =
File.GetLastAccessTime(@"C:\MyFile.txt");
```

C# Programming

```csharp
//get the last time the file was written
DateTime lastWriteTime =
File.GetLastWriteTime(@"C:\MyFile.txt");


// Transfer the file to a new location
File.Move(@"C:\MyFile.txt", @"D:\MyFile.txt");


//Open file and returns FileStream for reading
bytes from the file
FileStream fs = File.Open(@"D:\MyFile.txt",
FileMode.OpenOrCreate);


//Open the file and return a StreamReader for
reading a string from the file
StreamReader sr =
File.OpenText(@"D:\MyFile.txt");


//Delete the file
File.Delete(@"C:\MyFile.txt");
```

The above shows that with the Static File class, it becomes easy for us to work with physical files. However, for a more flexibility, one can use the *FileInfo* class.

StreamReader Class

This class helps us to read data from a text file. This class inherits the Stream base class. It also inherits the TextReader class, an abstract base class for reading a series of characters. The following are the popular methods provided by this class:

- public override void Close()- the method closes the StreamReader object and the stream, then any system resources that were being used by the reader are released.
- public override int Peek()- this method will return the next character that is available without consuming it.
- public override int Read()- this method will read the next character in an input stream then advance the position of the character by 1.

Let us demonstrate how we can use this class to read from a file named *names.txt*:

```
using System.IO;
using System;

namespace IOApplication {
    class MyProgram {
        static void Main(string[] args) {
            try {
```

```csharp
        // Create a StreamReader instance
for reading from a file.
        // The using statement will close
the StreamReader.
        using (StreamReader sr = new
StreamReader("c:/names.txt")) {
            string line;


            // Read the  show lines from the
file until
            // you reach the end of the file.
            while ((line = sr.ReadLine()) !=
null) {
                Console.WriteLine(line);
            }
        }
    } catch (Exception exception) {
        // Information the user about what
went wrong
            Console.WriteLine("File couldn't be
read:");

Console.WriteLine(exception.Message);
    }
        Console.ReadKey();
    }
  }
}
```

C# Programming

The code will read the text written in the file *names.txt* and print it.

StreamWriter Class

This class inherits the TextWriter abstract class that represents a write, capable of writing a series of characters. Here are the popular methods for this class:

- public override void Close()- this method will close the current object of the StreamWriter as well as the underlying stream.

- public override void Flush()- this method will clears buffers for current writer and makes any buffered data to be written to the stream.

- public virtual void Write(bool value)- this methods writes a textual representation of a Boolean value into the text stream or string.

- public override void Write(char value)- for writing a character to a stream.

- public virtual void Write(decimal value)- this method writes a textual representation of a decimal value to a text stream or string.

C# Programming

- public virtual void Write(double value)- writes a text representation of 8-byte floating point value into a text stream or string.

- public virtual void Write(int value)- writes a text representation of 4-byte signed integer into a text stream or string.

- public override void Write(string value)- for writing a string to a stream.

- public virtual void WriteLine()- for writing a line terminator to a text stream or string.

Let us demonstrate how we can use the StreamWriter class to write text data:

```csharp
using System.IO;
using System;
namespace IOApp {
    class MyProgram {
        static void Main(string[] args) {
            string[] students = new string[]
{"Nicholas Samuel", "Michelle Boss"};

            using (StreamWriter sw = new
StreamWriter("students.txt")) {

                foreach (string x in students) {
```

```
            sw.WriteLine(x);
    }
    }


    // Read and display every line from the
file.
    string text = "";
    using (StreamReader sr = new
StreamReader("students.txt")) {
        while ((text = sr.ReadLine()) !=
null) {
            Console.WriteLine(text);
        }
    }
    Console.ReadKey();
    }
    }
}
```

The code will print the following result after execution:

```
Nicholas Samuel
Michelle Boss
```

BinaryReader Class

This class can be used for reading binary data from a file. We should first create a BinaryReader object by passing an object of FileStream to its constructor. This class comes with a number of methods including the following:

- public override void Close()- for closing the BinaryReader object as well as the underlying stream.

- public virtual int Read()- for reading characters from underlying stream and advancing the stream's current position.

- public virtual bool ReadBoolean()- for reading a Boolean value from current stream and advancing the stream's current position by a byte.

- public virtual byte ReadByte()- for reading the next byte from current stream into byte array and advancing current position by a similar number of bytes.

BinaryWriter Class

This class helps in writing binary data into a stream. To create a BinaryWriter object, we pass a FileStream object to the constructor. This class comes with a number of methods including the following:

- public override void Close()- for closing the BinaryWriter object as well as the underlying stream.

- public virtual void Flush()-this method will clears buffers for current writer and makes any buffered data to be written to the device.

- public virtual void Write(bool value)- for writing a one-byte Boolean value into the current stream. 1 represents true while 0 represents false.

Let us create an example that demonstrates how to read and write binary data:

```csharp
using System;
using System.IO;
namespace BinaryFileApplication {
    class MyProgram {
        static void Main(string[] args) {
            BinaryWriter bw;
            BinaryReader br;

            int x = 12;
            double db = 1.24658;
            bool bl = false;
            string st = "Hello world";

            //create a file
            try {
```

C# Programming

```
        bw = new BinaryWriter(new
FileStream("testdata", FileMode.Create));
        } catch (IOException exception) {
            Console.WriteLine(exception.Message
+ "\n Unable to create the file.");
            return;
        }
        //write to the file
        try {
            bw.Write(x);
            bw.Write(db);
            bw.Write(bl);
            bw.Write(st);
        } catch (IOException exception) {
            Console.WriteLine(exception.Message
+ "\n Unable to write to the file.");
            return;
        }
        bw.Close();


        //read from the file
        try {
            br = new BinaryReader(new
FileStream("testdata", FileMode.Open));
        } catch (IOException exception) {
            Console.WriteLine(exception.Message
+ "\n Unable to open the file.");
```

```
            return;
        }
        try {
            x = br.ReadInt32();
            Console.WriteLine("Integer data:
{0}", x);
            db = br.ReadDouble();
            Console.WriteLine("Double data:
{0}", db);
            bl = br.ReadBoolean();
            Console.WriteLine("Boolean data:
{0}", bl);
            st = br.ReadString();
            Console.WriteLine("String data:
{0}", st);
        } catch (IOException exception) {
            Console.WriteLine(exception.Message
+ "\n Unable to read from the file.");
            return;
        }
        br.Close();
        Console.ReadKey();
    }
}
}
```

The code will give the following result after execution:

C# Programming

```
Integer data: 12
Double data: 1.24658
Boolean data: False
String data: Hello world
```

Chapter 18- Delegates

We can have a function with more than one parameters from different data types. However, we may sometimes need to pass a certain function as a parameter. How can C# handle the event handler or callback functions? This is done via *delegates*.

A delegate can be seen as a pointer to a function. It is a reference data type that holds reference of a method. All delegates are derived from *System.Delegate* class implicitly. We use delegates to implement events and call-back methods.

Declaring a Delegate

The way we declare a delegate determine the methods that the delegate can reference. A delegate may refer to a method, which has the same signature as the delegate. We use the *delegate* keyword to declare a delegate. The following syntax is used for the declaration:

```
<access modifier> delegate <return
type><delegate_name>(<parameters>)
```

Here is an example:

```
public delegate void Display(int value);
```

Above, we have declared a *Display* delegate. We can use this delegate to point to a method with same return type and parameters that have been declared with the *Display* delegate.

C# Programming

Consider the example given below:

```csharp
using System;
public class MyProgram
{
        public delegate void Display(int num);

        public static void Main()
        {
                // Display delegate points to the
DisplayNumber
                Display displayDel = DisplayNumber;

                displayDel(100000);
                displayDel(200);

                // Display delegate points to
DisplayMoney
                displayDel = DisplayMoney;

                displayDel(50000);
                displayDel(20);
        }

        public static void DisplayNumber(int x)
        {
```

```
        Console.WriteLine("Number: {0,-
12:N0}",x);
    }
    public static void DisplayMoney(int amount)
    {
        Console.WriteLine("Money: {0:C}",
amount);
    }
}
```

The code will print out the following:

```
Number: 100,000
Number: 200
Money: $50,000.00
Money: $20.00
```

We have created a delegate named *Display* that accepts a parameter of type integer and returns void. With the Main() method, we have created a variable of type Display and a method named *DisplayNumber* has been assigned to it. After invoking the Display delegate, the DisplayNumber method will be called also, if the Display delegate variable is assigned to DisplayMoney method, the DisplayMoney method will be invoked.

Also, it is possible for us to create a delegate object using the *new* keyword. In this case, we have to specify the name of the method as shown below:

C# Programming

```
Display displayDel = new Display
(DisplayNumber);
```

Invoking a Delegate

A delegate is a reference to a method; hence we can invoke it simply like a method. When a delegate is invoked, the method that is referred to will in turn be invoked.

There are two ways through which we can invoke a delegate: using the () operator or using *Invoke()* method of delegate. Let us demonstrate this using an example:

```
Display displayDel = DisplayNumber;
displayDel.Invoke(5000);
```

```
//or
printDel(10000);
```

The two ways that we can use to invoke a delegate have been shown above.

Passing a Delegate as a Parameter

A method may have a parameter of delegate type and it can invoke the delegate parameter. Here is an example of a delegate parameter:

```
public static void DisplayHelper(Display
delegateFunc, int numToDisplay)
{
```

```
        delegateFunc(numToDisplay);
}
```

In the example given above, the DisplayHelper function has a delegate parameter of Display type and it has been invoked as a function using the statement given below:

```
        delegateFunc(numToDisplay);
```

Let us give another example demonstrating how to use the *DisplayHelper* method and a delegate type parameter:

```
using System;

public class MyProgram
{
        public delegate void Display(int num);

        public static void Main()
        {
                DisplayHelper(DisplayNumber, 500);
            DisplayHelper(DisplayMoney, 200);
        }

        public static void DisplayHelper(Display
delegateFunc, int numToDisplay)
        {
            delegateFunc(numToDisplay);
        }
```

C# Programming

```
    public static void DisplayNumber(int val)
    {
        Console.WriteLine("Number: {0,-
12:N0}",val);
    }


    public static void DisplayMoney(int amount)
    {
        Console.WriteLine("Money: {0:C}",
amount);
    }
}
```

The code will return the following output:

```
Number: 500
Money: $200.00
```

Multicast Delegate

It is possible for a delegate to point to multiple functions. Any delegate that points to many functions is referred to as a *multicast delegate*. Use the + operator to add a function to a delegate object and the – operator to remove an existing function from a delegate object.

Consider the example given below:

```
using System;
```

```
public class MyProgram
{
        public delegate void Display(int value);

        public static void Main()
        {
                Display displayDel = DisplayNumber;
                displayDel += DisplayHexadecimal;
                displayDel += DisplayMoney;

                displayDel(1000);
                displayDel -= DisplayHexadecimal;
                displayDel(2000);
        }
        public static void DisplayNumber(int x)
        {
                Console.WriteLine("Number: {0,-
12:N0}",x);
        }


        public static void DisplayMoney(int
amount)
        {
                Console.WriteLine("Money: {0:C}",
amount);
        }
```

C# Programming

```
        public static void DisplayHexadecimal(int dec)
        {
                Console.WriteLine("Hexadecimal: {0:X}", dec);
        }
}
```

The code will print the following as the result:

```
Number: 1,000
Hexadecimal: 3E8
Money: $1,000.00
Number: 2,000
Money: $2,000.00
```

In the above example, we have the Display pointing to three methods namely DisplayNumber, DisplayMoney and DisplayHexadecimal. This makes it a multicast delegate. This means that when the displayDel is invoked, it will in turn invoke all the three methods sequentially.

Chapter 19- Events

An event is something that is expected to happen. In C#, events are user actions like click, key press, mouse movements or occurrences such as system generated notifications. Application should respond to events once they occur. A good example is the occurrence of an interrupt. Events are used to facilitate inter-process communications.

Events are declared in a class and associated with an event handler via delegates in the same class or in another class. The class with the event is used for publishing the event. Such is known as the *publisher* class. The class accepting the event is known as the *subscriber class*. This means that events rely on a publisher-subscriber model.

The publisher is the object with the definition of both the event and the delegate. The association between the event and the delegate is defined in this object. An object of the publisher class invokes the event which is in turn notified to the other objects.

The subscriber is the object that accepts the event and offers the event handler. The publisher class has a delegate that invokes the method (event handler) of subscriber class.

C# Programming

Event Declaration

For an event to be declared inside a class, you should first declare a delegate type for the event. It is after this that you can declare the event using the *event* keyword. Here is an example:

```
public delegate void myEvent();
public event myEvent myEvent;
```

Thus, we have used the *event* keyword to make it an event. Here is a complete example:

```
using System;
public class DisplayHelper
{
    // declare the delegate
    public delegate void BeforeDisplay();

    //declare an event of type delegate
    public event BeforeDisplay
beforeDisplayEvent;

    public DisplayHelper()
    {

    }

    public void DisplayNumber(int x)
```

```
    {
        //call the delegate method before moving
to display
        if (beforeDisplayEvent != null)
            beforeDisplayEvent();

        Console.WriteLine("Number: {0,-12:N0}",
x);
    }


    public void PrintDecimal(int dec)
    {
        if (beforeDisplayEvent != null)
            beforeDisplayEvent();

        Console.WriteLine("Decimal: {0:G}",
dec);
    }


    public void DisplayMoney(int amount)
    {
        if (beforeDisplayEvent != null)
            beforeDisplayEvent();

        Console.WriteLine("Money: {0:C}",
amount);
    }
```

C# Programming

```
    public void DisplayTemperature(int x)
    {
        if (beforeDisplayEvent != null)
            beforeDisplayEvent();

        Console.WriteLine("Temperature: {0,4:N1}
F", x);
    }
    public void DisplayHexadecimal(int dec)
    {
        if (beforeDisplayEvent != null)
            beforeDisplayEvent();

        Console.WriteLine("Hexadecimal: {0:X}",
dec);
    }
}
```

The *DisplayHelper* is a publisher class responsible for publishing the *beforeDisplay* event. After every *display* method, it first checks to determine whether the *beforeDisplayEvent* is not null then it calls the *beforeDisplayEvent()* method.

We now need to create a subscriber. Consider the class given below:

```
using System;
```

```csharp
public class MyProgram
{

    public static void Main()
    {
        NumberClass nc = new
NumberClass(200);
        nc.DisplayMoney();
        nc.DisplayNumber();
    }
}


class NumberClass
{
    private DisplayHelper _displayHelper;

    public NumberClass(int x)
    {
        _value = x;

        _displayHelper = new DisplayHelper();
        //subscribe to the beforeDisplayEvent
event
        _displayHelper.beforeDisplayEvent +=
displayHelper_beforeDisplayEvent;
    }
    //beforeDisplayevent handler
```

```csharp
    void displayHelper_beforeDisplayEvent()
    {

Console.WriteLine("BeforeDisplayEventHandler:
DisplayHelper will print a value");
    }

    private int _value;

    public int Value
    {
        get { return _value; }
        set { _value = value; }
    }

    public void DisplayMoney()
    {
        _displayHelper.DisplayMoney(_value);
    }

    public void DisplayNumber()
    {
        _displayHelper.DisplayNumber(_value);
    }
}
```

```csharp
public class DisplayHelper
{
    // declare a delegate
    public delegate void BeforeDisplay();

    //declare an event of type delegate
    public event BeforeDisplay
beforeDisplayEvent;

    public DisplayHelper()
    {

    }

    public void DisplayNumber(int y)
    {
    //call a delegate method before printing
        if (beforeDisplayEvent != null)
            beforeDisplayEvent();

        Console.WriteLine("Number: {0,-12:N0}",
y);
    }

    public void DisplayDecimal(int dec)
    {
```

```
        if (beforeDisplayEvent != null)
            beforeDisplayEvent();


        Console.WriteLine("Decimal: {0:G}",
dec);
    }


    public void DisplayMoney(int amount)
    {
        if (beforeDisplayEvent != null)
            beforeDisplayEvent();


        Console.WriteLine("Money: {0:C}",
amount);
    }


    public void DisplayTemperature(int y)
    {
        if (beforeDisplayEvent != null)
            beforeDisplayEvent();


        Console.WriteLine("Temperature: {0,4:N1}
F", y);
    }
    public void DisplayHexadecimal(int dc)
    {
        if (beforeDisplayEvent != null)
```

```
            beforeDisplayEvent();


        Console.WriteLine("Hexadecimal: {0:X}",
dc);

    }
}
```

The code returns the following result:

```
BeforeDisplayEventHandler: DisplayHelper will print a value
Money: $200.00
BeforeDisplayEventHandler: DisplayHelper will print a value
Number: 200
```

All subscribers must have a handler function which will be called after the publisher has raised an event.

C# Programming

Conclusion

This marks the end of this guide. C# is a compiled programming language developed by Microsoft. C# is also an object oriented programming language, meaning that it supports concepts like the use of classes, objects, inheritance, encapsulation, polymorphism etc. To program in C#, you need the .Net framework. This framework was also developed by Microsoft. You also need an integrated development environment (IDE). Visual studio is the common IDE used for programming in C#. You can get its free edition online. The .Net framework can only run on the Windows operating system. This means that if you are using Linux or Mac OS, you have to look for an alternative so as to be able to program in C#. You can use Mono, an open source framework that acts as an alternative to the .Net framework. It can be used on both Linux and Mac OS.

C# is an easy programming language, making it good even to the beginners in programming. One only needs to setup the environment and start writing and running their C# code. You can use C# alone to develop a complete computer application.

C# Programming

Thank you!

Thank you for buying this book! It is intended to help you understanding C# Programming. If you enjoyed this book and felt that it helped you learn C# Programming, please take the time to review it.

Your honest feedback would be greatly appreciated. It really does make a difference.

THE BEST WAY TO THANK AN AUTHOR IS TO WRITE REVIEW

C# Programming

Made in the USA
Lexington, KY
17 January 2019